THE DAILY LIFE OF THE GODLY WIFE

by

Madison Weatherly

1

ISBN: 979-8-218-81274-4

Publisher: Sprout Books

Contents

This book is lovingly dedicated to my dearest husband, my partner in

faith and life, whose unwavering love and support form the very

foundation of our home and family. To our precious children, the

vibrant heartbeats of our household, whose laughter and boundless

energy fill our days with purpose and joy. May this journey of

spiritual growth and homemaking inspire us all to continually seek

God's presence, to nurture a love that deepens with each passing

year, and to build a legacy of faith that will echo through generations.

Your lives are a testament to God's faithfulness, and it is for your

flourishing, both spiritually and physically, that I pour my heart into

these pages. May our home always be a sanctuary of His peace and a

beacon of His love.

Introduction

In the tapestry of a woman's life, especially as a wife and mother, the threads of faith, home, and family are intricately woven together. This book is born from a deep desire to explore and nurture these sacred connections, particularly for women navigating the beautiful, yet often demanding, seasons of raising a family or anticipating one. It is a gentle invitation to step into the profound calling of creating a home that is not just a dwelling place, but a vibrant sanctuary where God's presence is keenly felt, and where love, peace, and spiritual growth are cultivated daily. We live in a world that can pull us in countless directions, often leaving us feeling depleted or overwhelmed. My own journey has revealed the immense power of intentionality, of grounding our daily practices in the timeless wisdom of Scripture and in a deeper reliance on our Heavenly Father. This guide is designed to offer practical, actionable steps – from nurturing our bodies with wholesome food to strengthening our marriages and raising our children in faith. It's about re-framing the mundane tasks of homemaking into opportunities for spiritual connection, for discipleship, and for experiencing God's grace in the everyday moments. My prayer is that this resource will equip you, encourage you, and inspire you to embrace the transformative potential within your home, fostering an atmosphere that reflects the heart of God and leaves a lasting legacy of faith and love for your family.

The concept of a "godly home" is not an abstract ideal whispered only in hushed tones, but a living, breathing reality that can be actively cultivated by every believing wife and mother. This book is an exploration of that journey, a companion for women seeking to infuse their daily lives with spiritual purpose and to build a domestic haven rooted in faith, love, and intentionality. In a world that often prioritizes outward success and fleeting trends, we are called to a deeper, more enduring legacy – the shaping of hearts and souls within the intimate sphere of our homes. This guide is crafted for you, the woman who desires more than just a clean house, but a home that is a true sanctuary, a place where her husband and children can find rest, encouragement, and a tangible connection to the divine. We will delve into practical strategies for nurturing our own well-being, both physically and spiritually, recognizing that our own vitality is the wellspring from which we pour into our families. We will explore how the rhythms of daily, weekly, and monthly practices can create sacred moments, strengthening our bonds with our spouses and children, and deepening our walk with God. From the nourishment of our bodies through mindful eating and movement to the intentional cultivation of a strong marriage and the joyful task of raising children in the ways of the Lord, every aspect of our homemaking can become an act of worship and a conduit for God's grace. Consider this an invitation to see your home not just as a responsibility, but as a sacred trust, a place where the love of Christ can shine brightly, transforming the ordinary into the extraordinary and building a foundation of faith that will stand the test of time.

Chapter 1: Laying the Foundation – A Godly Home

In the tapestry of life, woven with threads of joy, challenge, and divine purpose, the roles of wife and mother stand as particularly sacred callings. Far from being mere societal constructs or mundane duties, these vocations are imbued with profound spiritual significance. Understanding this biblical perspective is the cornerstone upon which a godly home is built, transforming everyday tasks into acts of worship and service that honor God. It's about recognizing that the work of stewarding a home, loving a husband, and nurturing children is not insignificant, but rather a divinely appointed mission, a testament to God's grace and wisdom.

The Scriptures repeatedly affirm the value and honor bestowed upon women who embrace their roles with love, diligence, and wisdom. Proverbs 31, often referred to as the "virtuous woman" passage, paints a vivid picture of a woman whose worth extends far beyond superficial appearances. She is industrious, wise, and compassionate. Her hands are busy, her heart is generous, and her influence extends to her family and community. This passage isn't meant to create an impossible standard, but rather to illuminate the potential and inherent dignity in the work of a wife and mother. It shows us a woman who is respected not just by her family, but who also commands respect through her actions and character. She is celebrated not for worldly achievements, but for her godly character and her faithful stewardship of her home and her resources. This ancient text still resonates today because it speaks to the deep-seated human desire for purpose and significance, assuring us that the labor of love within the home is indeed honorable in God's eyes.

When we accept these roles with a willing and surrendered heart, we open the door for God's presence to permeate our homes. It's a choice to view our tasks not through the lens of exhaustion or obligation, but through the lens of faith, recognizing that God can use even the most mundane activities to reflect His glory. Think of the simple act of preparing a meal. When done with a heart focused on nourishing your family, both physically and spiritually, it becomes an offering. When you fold laundry with an attitude of creating a comfortable and loving environment for your husband and children, it's an act of service that pleases God. This shift in perspective is foundational. It's the first step in transforming your house into a sanctuary, a place where God's peace and love are palpable. It's about intentionally infusing your home with His spirit, making it a haven of rest and spiritual growth.

The Bible calls us to be diligent in our homes, to manage them with wisdom. This isn't about perfection, but about a diligent heart. The book of Titus, chapter 2, verses 4-5, speaks to older women teaching the younger women to love their husbands and children, to be self-controlled, pure, working at home, kind, and subject to their own husbands, so that the word of God may not be reviled. While the specific age reference might differ, the principle remains: the faithful stewardship of the home is a testament to God's word. It's a reflection of His order, His love, and His provision. When we embrace this, we are not just tending to a physical space; we are cultivating a spiritual atmosphere. We are building a legacy of faith, one day, one task, one prayer at a time.

Furthermore, understanding our divine calling helps us to resist the insidious whispers of comparison and inadequacy that so often plague modern women. In a world saturated with curated images and impossible expectations, it's easy to feel like we're falling short. But God's calling on our lives as wives and mothers is unique and sovereign. It's not meant to be measured against anyone else's. When we anchor our identity in Christ, recognizing that our worth is not dependent on our performance as wives or mothers, but on His finished work on the cross, we find true freedom. This secure identity becomes the wellspring of our strength, enabling us to serve our families from a place of abundance, not depletion.

Consider the impact of this understanding on our daily routines. When we see washing dishes as an act of caring for the home God has entrusted to us, or when we read a bedtime story as an opportunity to sow seeds of faith into our children's hearts, these actions take on a new dimension. They become sacred, not simply chores. This spiritual mindset allows us to approach even the most repetitive tasks with renewed purpose and joy. It's about seeing the divine in the domestic. It's about recognizing that the love we pour into our homes, the patience we extend to our husbands and children, the wisdom we seek in managing our households – these are all offerings to the Lord.

The Bible teaches us that our bodies are temples of the Holy Spirit (1 Corinthians 6:19-20). This principle extends to the stewardship of our homes. A well-ordered, peaceful home environment contributes significantly to the spiritual and emotional well-being of its inhabitants. When we intentionally create a welcoming and tranquil space, we are, in essence, reflecting God's character and inviting His presence. This isn't about achieving Pinterest-perfect aesthetics; it's about cultivating an atmosphere of peace, love, and order that speaks of God's gracious nature. Even amidst the inevitable chaos of family life, small, intentional acts can make a profound difference. A clean kitchen counter after a busy day, a quiet corner for prayer, a warm embrace – these are all threads in the fabric of a God-centered home.

Embracing our calling as wives and mothers is a journey of faith, a continuous process of learning and growth. It requires us to lean into God's strength, to seek His wisdom, and to trust in His unfailing love. By understanding the spiritual significance of our roles, we can move beyond the demands of the world and embrace the divine purpose God has for us, building homes that are not only beautiful and functional, but are also rich in faith, hope, and love. This foundational understanding is the true bedrock upon which a thriving, godly home is built. It sets the tone for everything that follows, empowering us with a renewed sense of purpose and dignity in every aspect of our lives. It is from this place of spiritual understanding that we can truly begin to lay the foundation for a home that honors God in all its facets.

When we understand that our roles are a divine calling, it reframes our entire perspective on homemaking and family life. It's no longer just about managing a household; it's about stewarding a sacred trust, a place where God's presence is meant to dwell. The scriptures are rich with examples of women who honored God through their faithfulness in their homes. Think of Sarah, the wife of Abraham, who, despite her own imperfections, was part of a lineage that God used to bring about His redemptive plan. Or consider the women mentioned in the New Testament who supported Jesus and the apostles in their ministry, often through their hospitality and provision within their homes. These women, though their specific circumstances differed, all embodied a spirit of faithful service and dedication that honored God.

The Apostle Paul, in his letter to Timothy, emphasizes the value of godly womanhood, particularly within the context of family and faith. In 1 Timothy 5:8, he states, "Anyone who does not provide for their relatives, and especially for their own household, has denied the faith and is worse than an unbeliever." This is a strong declaration, highlighting the responsibility that comes with our roles. However, the flip side, the positive aspect, is equally profound. When we faithfully provide for and nurture our households, we are, in essence, living out our faith. We are demonstrating God's provision and love in a tangible way. This isn't about a burden, but about an opportunity to reflect the character of a God who cares deeply for His creation and His family.

The value placed on women in biblical culture was often intrinsically tied to their role within the home. While this might seem foreign to our modern sensibilities, which often prioritize external achievements, it's crucial to understand the depth of honor associated with skillful and loving homemaking in that context. A woman who managed her household well, who provided for her family, who created a place of refuge and love, was a pillar of her community. Her wisdom and diligence were highly esteemed. This historical and biblical context should encourage us, reminding us that God sees and values the work we do within our homes, even when it goes unnoticed by the world. It's a call to embrace this inherent dignity, to see our responsibilities not as limitations, but as avenues for expressing God's love and faithfulness.

Moreover, embracing this calling with a willing heart means actively choosing to see our homes as places of ministry. Just as a pastor ministers to a congregation or a missionary ministers to a distant land, we minister to the most intimate and foundational unit of society – our families. This ministry is vital and impactful. It shapes character, instills values, and creates the environment where faith can flourish. When we approach our homes with this mindset, we are consciously inviting God to work through us. We are asking Him to infuse our efforts with His strength and His wisdom. This intentionality is key. It transforms the mundane into the magnificent, the ordinary into the extraordinary, because it is infused with the divine.

This understanding also serves as a powerful antidote to the cultural narrative that often dismisses or devalues the work of homemaking and mothering. In a society that frequently glorifies career advancement and public recognition, the quiet, consistent work within the home can be overlooked. But God's perspective is different. He sees the heart behind the effort. He values the love poured into raising children and nurturing a family. By embracing our divine calling, we align ourselves with God's perspective, finding deep satisfaction and purpose in the work He has set before us. This is not about conforming to worldly standards, but about embracing a higher calling, a heavenly perspective on our earthly responsibilities.

The initial step in building a godly home is recognizing that it is built upon a foundation of faith, and that our roles within that home are divinely appointed. When we understand the spiritual significance and inherent purpose in being a wife and mother, we are empowered. We are equipped with a renewed sense of dignity and purpose in our daily tasks. This foundational understanding is what allows us to move forward with confidence, knowing that we are not alone in this endeavor, but are partnered with God Himself. It fosters a spiritual mindset from the outset, shaping our actions, our attitudes, and the very atmosphere of our homes. It's a declaration that our homes are not just places of living, but places where God is honored, where His love is cultivated, and where His presence is welcomed and cherished. This is the true beginning of laying the foundation for a godly home.

The transformation of our homes from mere living spaces into sacred environments is a profound journey, one that begins with a fundamental shift in perspective. It is about recognizing that the atmosphere we cultivate within our homes has a direct and powerful impact on the spiritual well-being of every person who dwells there. This is not a call to sterile perfection or an unattainable ideal, but rather an invitation to imbue our domestic spaces with intention, love, and the palpable presence of God. When we cease to view our homes as simply a collection of rooms where chores are performed and instead see them as a sanctuary where faith is nurtured, lived out, and where God's presence is welcomed, we begin to lay the bedrock of a truly godly home.

Consider the intentionality with which we might prepare a sacred space for worship or study. We might tidy the area, ensure good lighting, perhaps light a candle, and create an atmosphere of reverence. This same intentionality, applied to our homes, can elevate the ordinary into the extraordinary. It's about recognizing that the very air within our homes can be saturated with peace, love, and joy, or it can be heavy with stress, disorder, and conflict. The choice, and the power to influence that atmosphere, rests with us as the keepers of the home. This is where the practical application of our faith truly shines, demonstrating that holiness is not confined to church walls, but is meant to permeate every aspect of our lives, including the very walls of our dwellings.

The Bible consistently speaks of peace and order as attributes of God's kingdom. When we strive to bring these qualities into our homes, we are, in essence, inviting a tangible manifestation of His reign into our daily lives. This doesn't mean our homes must be immaculate at all times, or that the sounds of children's laughter and play are unwelcome. Rather, it speaks to the underlying spirit with which we manage our households. A home where peace is actively sought, where disagreements are handled with grace, and where love is the prevailing currency, becomes a sanctuary. It's a place where souls can find rest, where spirits can be refreshed, and where a deep sense of security and belonging is fostered. This is particularly crucial for our children, whose formative years are so profoundly shaped by the environment in which they grow. A peaceful home is a safe harbor, a place where they can explore, learn, and develop their faith without undue anxiety or internal conflict.

Creating this sacred atmosphere begins with small, intentional acts. It's in the welcoming greeting at the door after a long day. It's in the mindful preparation of meals, not just as fuel, but as an act of love and nourishment. It's in the way we arrange our living spaces, creating areas of comfort and connection. It might be a designated quiet corner for prayer and reflection, a tidy space for children's activities that encourages focus, or simply ensuring that the common areas of the home are inviting and conducive to spending time together. These are not grand gestures, but consistent, daily choices that speak volumes about what we value and what we are seeking to cultivate. The cumulative effect of these small acts builds a powerful spiritual momentum within the home.

Think about the concept of hospitality, a theme that runs deeply through Scripture. True hospitality is more than just inviting people over; it's about creating an environment where others feel welcomed, loved, and at ease. When we extend this same spirit of hospitality to our own family members, we are actively building the sacredness of our homes. It means making our husbands and children feel truly seen, heard, and cherished within the space we share. It's about creating an atmosphere where they feel safe to be vulnerable, to share their joys and their struggles, and to know they are unconditionally loved. This intentionality in welcoming and cherishing those closest to us is a cornerstone of a God-centered home.

The state of our homes often reflects the state of our hearts. When we feel overwhelmed, stressed, or disconnected from God, our homes can often mirror that internal chaos. Conversely, when we are seeking God, intentionally cultivating peace, and nurturing our relationships, our homes can become vibrant expressions of His presence. This highlights the importance of our own spiritual discipline. A wife and mother who prioritizes her relationship with God, who seeks His wisdom and strength, is far better equipped to create a sacred and peaceful home environment. This isn't about adding more to an already full plate, but about reordering our priorities, recognizing that our spiritual vitality directly fuels our ability to steward our homes well.

The Apostle Paul exhorts us in Philippians 4:8 to think about whatever is true, noble, right, pure, lovely, admirable, excellent, or praiseworthy. This verse offers a powerful lens through which to view our homemaking. When we focus on these qualities in our thoughts, our conversations, and our actions within the home, we naturally begin to cultivate an atmosphere that reflects them. This means choosing to speak words of encouragement rather than criticism, to seek solutions rather than dwelling on problems, and to actively look for the good and the beautiful in our family life and our surroundings. It's a conscious decision to bring the light of Christ into the domestic sphere.

Consider the impact of order and cleanliness, not as an end in itself, but as a means to foster peace and reflect God's nature. While perfection is not the goal, a reasonable level of order can significantly reduce stress and create a more serene environment. It can be as simple as establishing routines for tidying up at the end of the day, teaching children to put away their toys, or ensuring that meals are prepared and eaten in a somewhat organized fashion. These routines, established with grace and consistency, create a sense of predictability and calm that is incredibly beneficial for everyone in the household. They communicate a sense of care and respect for the shared space.

The Scriptures tell us in 1 Corinthians 14:33 that "God is not a God of disorder but of peace." This principle extends to the very fabric of our homes. While life with children is inherently dynamic and can sometimes feel chaotic, we can still strive for an underlying sense of order and peace. This might involve designating specific places for items, creating clear expectations for family members regarding household responsibilities, or establishing consistent mealtimes. These structures provide a sense of security and predictability, allowing for greater peace to flourish. It's about creating rhythms that honor God's nature of order and peace, rather than succumbing to the constant potential for disorder.

Moreover, the emotional climate of a home is deeply influenced by the way we manage conflict and express emotions. When disagreements arise, and they inevitably will, how we navigate them is paramount. Do we resort to harsh words, silent treatment, or escalating anger? Or do we strive to address issues with humility, seeking to understand, forgive, and reconcile? The latter approach cultivates a home where emotional safety is paramount, a key component of its sacredness. When family members know that disagreements can be resolved with love and respect, they feel more secure and connected. This intentionality in resolving conflict, in choosing grace over harshness, is a powerful act of spiritual stewardship within the home.

Think about the impact of our personal attitudes on the overall atmosphere. A spirit of gratitude, even in the midst of challenges, can be contagious. When we consciously choose to express thankfulness for our homes, our families, and the blessings God has provided, we shift the emotional tone from one of complaint to one of joy. This doesn't mean ignoring difficulties, but rather choosing to focus on God's faithfulness and provision, even when circumstances are not ideal. Practicing gratitude, perhaps through a family gratitude jar or simply by expressing thanks at mealtimes, can transform the prevailing mood of the household.

The creation of a sacred home environment is also deeply intertwined with the way we care for ourselves. When we are depleted, exhausted, and running on empty, it becomes significantly harder to cultivate peace and joy. Prioritizing our own spiritual, emotional, and physical well-being is not selfish; it is essential for our ability to minister effectively within our homes. This might involve ensuring adequate rest, finding moments for personal prayer and reflection, nourishing our bodies with healthy food, and engaging in activities that refresh our souls. When we are well, we are better equipped to pour into our families and create the kind of home environment that honors God.

Let us not underestimate the power of sensory experiences in shaping the atmosphere of our homes. The gentle glow of lamplight in the evening, the scent of baking bread, the sound of worship music playing softly in the background, or the simple beauty of fresh flowers – these elements can all contribute to a feeling of peace and sacredness. These are not frivolous additions, but intentional choices to create a space that nourishes the soul and points to the goodness of God. Even in the midst of a busy, active household, creating pockets of sensory beauty can offer moments of respite and a reminder of the divine.

Consider the spiritual significance of cleanliness and tidiness as an act of worship. When we clean our homes, not out of obligation or a desire for perfection, but as a way of honoring the space God has given us and caring for the people, He has placed within it, this mundane task becomes an offering. It is a tangible way of demonstrating our love and stewardship. A clean kitchen, a tidy living room, or a well-ordered bedroom can contribute to a sense of calm and well-being, allowing for greater focus on spiritual matters and deeper connection with family members. It's about approaching these tasks with a consecrated heart, seeing them as expressions of our faith and devotion.

The Bible speaks of the home as a place of refuge. In a world that can often feel overwhelming and chaotic, our homes should be sanctuaries of peace, safety, and love. This requires intentional effort. It means actively working to mitigate sources of stress and conflict, creating clear boundaries where necessary, and fostering an environment where every family member feels secure and cherished. This extends to our relationships with our husbands and children; it means prioritizing quality time, open communication, and a consistent demonstration of love and affection. A home that truly functions as a sanctuary is one where hearts can heal, spirits can be restored, and faith can flourish.

The quiet moments within the home are often the most powerful. The shared cup of tea with a child before bed, the brief conversation with a husband over breakfast, the few minutes spent in prayer before the day begins – these seemingly small instances are the building blocks of a sacred home. They are opportunities to connect, to nurture, and to infuse the day with God's presence. It is in these unhurried moments that the true work of building a godly home takes place, one intentional act of love at a time. These moments, when cultivated with care, become the threads that weave a strong tapestry of faith and family.

When we consider the profound impact of our homes on our spiritual lives and the lives of our families, the importance of cultivating a sacred atmosphere becomes undeniable. It is a calling, a privilege, and a responsibility that God has entrusted to us. By shifting our perspective, embracing intentionality in our daily routines, prioritizing peace and order, and consistently seeking God's presence, we can transform our houses into true sanctuaries of faith, love, and rest. This is the foundation upon which a truly godly home is built, a place where His glory can shine forth in every aspect of our lives. It is in this sacred space that our families can truly thrive, rooted in the unshakable love of Christ. This ongoing commitment to creating a spiritual haven is an act of worship in itself, a testament to our desire to honor God in the most intimate and foundational unit of society: our homes. It is here that the seeds of faith are sown, watered, and nurtured, creating a legacy that extends far beyond the physical walls of our dwellings.

Discovering your identity in Christ is not merely a theological concept; it is the bedrock upon which a life of purpose, peace, and effective service is built. Before we can fully embrace the roles of wife and mother, and before we can pour ourselves into nurturing a godly home, we must first understand who *we* are in the eyes of our Creator. Our identity is not found in our accomplishments, our family roles, our physical appearance, or even the approval of others. These are shifting sands, prone to erosion and disappointment. True, unwavering identity is found exclusively in Jesus Christ, our Lord and Savior. This truth is the unshakeable foundation that will sustain us through the joys and inevitable challenges of homemaking, marriage, and motherhood.

The world often bombards us with messages about worth, frequently tying it to productivity, external beauty, or social status. We can easily fall prey to this insidious lie, believing that our value is contingent upon how much we achieve, how perfect our homes look, or how flawlessly we manage our families. This external validation is a hollow pursuit, destined to leave us feeling empty and perpetually striving for an unreachable standard. The antidote to this worldly pressure lies in the divine affirmation that washes over us when we truly grasp our identity in Christ. The Bible is replete with declarations of our inherent worth, not earned by us, but freely given by God through His boundless love.

Consider the profound truth proclaimed in Ephesians 1:4-5: "For he chose us in him before the creation of the world to be holy and blameless in his sight. In love he predestined us for adoption to be his children through Jesus Christ, according to the good pleasure of his will." This verse alone is a powerful declaration of our identity. We were not an afterthought; we were chosen
before the foundation of the world. This wasn't a decision made based on our potential or our future good deeds. It was a choice rooted in God's eternal love and His sovereign purpose. To be chosen by God, predestined for adoption as His children, means we are deeply loved, eternally valued, and belong to Him. This is not a conditional love; it is a love that has been present from the very beginning. Our worth is therefore intrinsic, bestowed by the One who created the universe.

Furthermore, in 2 Corinthians 5:17, the Apostle Paul reminds us, "Therefore, if anyone is in Christ, the new creation has come: The old has gone, the new is here!" When we accept Jesus Christ as our Savior, we are not simply reformed; we are
recreated. Our past sins and failures are washed away, and we are given a new nature. This transformation is radical. It means our identity is no longer defined by who we *were*, but by who we *are* in Christ. This new identity is characterized by righteousness, grace, and the indwelling presence of the Holy Spirit. It is a constant state of being, regardless of our daily circumstances or our personal feelings. This is the essence of our redeemed identity – a perfect standing before God, made possible through Christ's sacrifice.

Understanding this new identity is crucial for navigating the demands of family life without succumbing to burnout or resentment. When our service stems from a deep well of God's love and our own secure identity in Him, it flows freely and joyfully. We are not performing to earn God's favor or to prove our worth. Instead, we are responding to the love He has already lavished upon us. This perspective shifts our motivation from obligation to overflow. When we feel empty, depleted, or unappreciated, it is often a sign that we are trying to draw from our own limited resources, rather than from the inexhaustible supply that is found in Christ.

The temptation to measure our worth by our performance is a subtle but pervasive spiritual attack. We might feel like a failure if the house isn't perfectly clean, if the children are misbehaving, or if our marriage hits a rough patch. These are often moments where the enemy whispers lies, telling us we are not good enough, not capable enough, or not loved enough. However, our identity in Christ liberates us from this cycle of performance-based validation. In God's eyes, we are already declared righteous, accepted, and deeply cherished, not because we are perfect, but because Christ is perfect for us. Romans 8:1 powerfully states, "Therefore, there is now no condemnation for those who are in Christ Jesus." This is a foundational truth. No amount of failure or imperfection can change our standing before God.

This understanding of our identity also helps us to gracefully receive grace, both from God and from our loved ones. When we know our worth is secure in Christ, we can acknowledge our mistakes without being crushed by them. We can offer forgiveness to others more readily because we have experienced the profound forgiveness of God. Our capacity to love and serve becomes less about our own efforts and more about reflecting the love that has transformed us. It allows us to approach our wifely and maternal duties not as burdens to be endured, but as opportunities to express the love and grace we have received.

Moreover, this deep-seated identity in Christ equips us to lead our homes with spiritual authority and wisdom. When we understand our position as beloved daughters of the King, we are empowered to raise our children in a way that honors Him. Our confidence in God's provision and His plan for our families allows us to navigate challenges with faith rather than fear. It means teaching our children about their own identity in Christ, grounding them in the same secure foundation that sustains us. We become conduits of God's love, reflecting His character in our homes, rather than striving to project an image of personal perfection.

It is essential to actively cultivate this awareness of our identity in Christ. This involves a conscious and consistent effort to immerse ourselves in God's Word, where these truths are revealed. Daily prayer and meditation on scripture are not optional extras; they are vital disciplines for reinforcing our spiritual identity. When we regularly remind ourselves of who God says we are, those truths begin to penetrate our hearts and minds, gradually displacing the lies of the world and our own internal critics. It is a process of renewing our minds, as Romans 12:2 encourages: "Do not conform to the pattern of this world but be transformed by the renewing of your mind. Then you will be able to test and approve what God's will is—his good, pleasing and perfect will."

Consider the concept of adoption mentioned earlier. In ancient Roman culture, adoption was a profound legal and familial act. An adopted child was not just taken in; they were fully integrated into the family, inheriting all the rights and privileges of a biological child, often even superseding natural heirs in legal standing. This is the depth of the spiritual adoption God has given us. We are not merely guests in His house; we are full heirs, joint heirs with Christ, positioned to receive all the promises and blessings He has prepared. This is the security that anchors us. Our identity is rooted in this unbreakable relationship.

This understanding also frees us from unhealthy comparisons with other women. Social media, in particular, can be a breeding ground for comparison, showcasing curated versions of life that often highlight success and happiness while obscuring the struggles. When we are insecure about our identity, we are more susceptible to feeling inadequate when we see others who appear to have it all together. But when our primary identity is in Christ, we can celebrate the gifts and callings God has given to others without feeling diminished. We recognize that God has uniquely designed and purposed each of us, and our worth is not diminished by the blessings He bestows on others.

The practical application of this truth is profound. When we know we are deeply loved and accepted by God, we are more likely to extend grace to ourselves. We can embrace imperfection as part of the human experience, trusting that God's grace is sufficient for our shortcomings. This self-compassion, rooted in divine love, is essential for avoiding the burnout that so often plagues women who are trying to do it all and be it all without relying on God's strength. It allows us to rest, to recharge, and to approach our responsibilities with renewed vigor, knowing that our ultimate acceptance does not hinge on our performance.

Furthermore, this secure identity empowers us to set healthy boundaries. When we understand our value and purpose, we are less likely to overcommit or allow others to deplete our energy without regard for our well-being. We can say no when necessary, prioritize our spiritual and emotional health, and protect the sacred space of our homes from undue intrusion. This is not selfishness; it is wise stewardship of the resources God has given us, including our own physical and emotional capacity.

The journey of discovering and living out our identity in Christ is a lifelong process. It requires intentionality, a willingness to challenge ingrained beliefs, and a deep reliance on the Holy Spirit to reveal God's truth to our hearts. As we anchor ourselves in who God says we are – chosen, beloved, redeemed, and adopted – we lay the most critical foundation for creating a godly home. This inner security, this unwavering sense of belonging in Him, is the vital fuel that will sustain our efforts to nurture a thriving spiritual environment for our husbands and children. Without this grounding, our homemaking efforts can easily become a source of stress and weariness, rather than a joyful expression of God's love.

Therefore, before we delve into the specifics of wifely duties, maternal responsibilities, or the organization of our homes, let us first turn inward, to the unwavering truth of our identity in Christ. Let us spend time in His Word, in prayer, and in quiet reflection, allowing Him to reaffirm His love and acceptance of us. When we are firmly rooted in this truth, our service will be motivated by love, sustained by His strength, and ultimately bring glory to His name, transforming our homes into true sanctuaries of His presence and peace. This foundational understanding is not a mere prerequisite; it is the very essence of building a life and a home that reflects God's enduring love and faithfulness. It is the essential first step in becoming the woman God has called us to be, a woman who can, with grace and confidence, build a legacy of faith within her home. This deeply personal revelation will empower us to approach every aspect of our domestic lives with a profound sense of purpose and unwavering peace, knowing that our true worth is eternally secured in Him, regardless of the passing seasons of life or the changing tides of our circumstances.

The foundational understanding of our identity in Christ, as previously explored, serves as the bedrock for everything that follows in building a godly home. Yet, this identity is not merely a static declaration; it is a living truth that must be actively cultivated through a vibrant, personal relationship with God. This intimacy, this ongoing communion, is the wellspring from which all effective ministry within our homes flows. Without this deep, abiding connection, our efforts to create a spiritual atmosphere for our families can easily become hollow performances, driven by obligation rather than the overflow of a heart truly connected to the Divine. It is in this personal relationship that we discover the strength, wisdom, and unconditional love necessary to navigate the beautiful complexities of family life.

Nurturing this personal relationship is not a passive endeavor; it requires intentionality and the diligent practice of spiritual disciplines. At the forefront of these disciplines is prayer. Prayer is far more than a ritualistic recitation of words; it is a conversation, a direct line of communication with the Creator of the universe. It is in prayer that we lay bare our hearts, confess our weaknesses, express our gratitude, and seek His guidance for every facet of our lives, including the nurturing of our homes. Imagine approaching God not as a distant judge, but as a loving Father who yearns to hear from His children. When we pray, we are invited into His presence, where burdens are lightened, fears are dispelled, and wisdom is freely given. It is in these moments of unburdening ourselves, of sharing our joys and our struggles, that we truly begin to know Him and to be known by Him.

Beyond vocal prayer, there is the practice of meditating on Scripture. The Bible is not merely a collection of ancient texts; it is God's living Word, imbued with His Spirit and His truth. When we immerse ourselves in its pages, we are not just reading words on a page; we are engaging with God's very thoughts and intentions for us. Meditation is the process of taking a passage of Scripture and allowing it to sink deep into our hearts and minds. It involves reading slowly, reflecting on the meaning, asking questions of the text, and considering how it applies to our lives. For instance, when we read a passage about God's faithfulness, we can spend time reflecting on His faithfulness in our own lives, recalling specific instances where He has been true to His promises. This practice transforms the Word from an intellectual exercise into a deeply personal encounter, shaping our perspectives and aligning our hearts with God's will.

Another vital element in cultivating this personal relationship is the practice of quiet reflection. In our fast-paced, often noisy world, finding moments of stillness can feel like a monumental challenge. However, these moments of quiet are invaluable for spiritual growth. They are opportunities to simply
be with God, to listen to His voice amidst the internal and external clamor. This might involve sitting quietly with a cup of tea in the morning before the household awakens, taking a few minutes during a child's nap, or even stealing a few moments in the car before entering the house after an errand. During these times, we can focus on God's presence, allowing His peace to wash over us. It is in this stillness that we are most likely to discern His gentle whispers, His promptings, and His direction.

The question often arises: how can busy wives and mothers possibly carve out time for these spiritual disciplines? The reality is, it's not about finding large, uninterrupted blocks of time, but about making these practices a priority, even in small increments. Consider the concept of "grace at the gate." This refers to finding small pockets of time, perhaps just five or ten minutes, to connect with God before diving into the day's responsibilities. This might mean waking up a little earlier, even if it's just fifteen minutes before the alarm is set to go off. It's about being disciplined enough to honor God with the first fruits of our day, recognizing that this investment will yield dividends throughout the hours that follow.

We can also integrate spiritual practices into our daily routines. While preparing meals, we can listen to a Christian podcast or an audiobook of a devotional. During household chores, we can play worship music and sing along, turning the mundane into a time of adoration. When driving, we can use that time for prayer or listening to Scripture readings. It's about transforming ordinary moments into opportunities for communion with God, recognizing that His presence is not confined to a particular time or place. This holistic approach ensures that our relationship with Him permeates every aspect of our lives, rather than being relegated to a scheduled appointment that can easily be missed.

The benefits of this intimate relationship with God are profound and far-reaching, particularly as they impact our roles within the home. When our hearts are filled with God's presence, we naturally overflow with His love. This love is not conditional; it is a steadfast, unwavering affection that enables us to love our husbands and children even when they are difficult, unappreciative, or simply having a bad day. It's the kind of love that forgives readily, that extends grace generously, and that perseveres through challenges. Without this divine source of love, our own emotional reserves can quickly become depleted, leading to frustration, resentment, and a sense of being overwhelmed. But when we are drawing from the inexhaustible well of God's love, we are empowered to love sacrificially and joyfully.

Furthermore, this intimacy cultivates a profound sense of resilience. The journey of homemaking and motherhood is rarely without its trials. There will be sleepless nights, unexpected illnesses, financial strains, and moments of deep disappointment. In these times, a personal relationship with God provides an anchor. Knowing that we are deeply loved and supported by the Almighty gives us the strength to endure, to press on, and to find hope even in the midst of adversity. It reminds us that our circumstances do not define our worth or our future, and that God is always working, even when we cannot see His hand at work.

Wisdom is another critical fruit of a close walk with God. As we seek

26

His face in prayer and immerse ourselves in His Word, He grants us discernment and insight into the complex decisions that arise in family life. He guides our parenting choices, offers wisdom in resolving conflicts with our spouses, and helps us to manage our homes effectively. This wisdom is not merely intellectual; it is a God-given understanding that enables us to navigate life's challenges with grace and prudence. It's the ability to see beyond the immediate situation and to make choices that honor God and build up our families in truth and love.

The ability to hear and respond to God's voice is perhaps one of the most precious aspects of this cultivated relationship. The Holy Spirit is our constant companion and advocate, guiding us into all truth. As we quiet ourselves and draw near to God, we become more attuned to His voice. This voice may come as a gentle nudge, a clear impression, a biblical verse that comes to mind, or an inner conviction. It is essential to distinguish God's voice from our own thoughts or the whispers of the enemy. Consistent engagement with Scripture and prayer builds our spiritual discernment, enabling us to recognize and follow His leading. When we are sensitive to His voice, we can respond with obedience, trusting that He knows what is best for us and our families.

Consider the practical application of hearing God's voice in the context of daily homemaking. Perhaps you are struggling with a particular child's behavior, and you've tried everything you can think of. In a moment of prayer and reflection, you might feel a strong impression to approach the situation with patience and a specific word of encouragement, rather than discipline. Or perhaps you are feeling overwhelmed by household tasks, and in a quiet moment, you sense God prompting you to delegate a certain responsibility to your older child, or to simply embrace imperfection for the day and rest. These are not random thoughts; they are often God's gentle invitations to walk in His wisdom and grace.

Cultivating this intimate relationship is an ongoing journey, not a destination. There will be seasons of spiritual dryness, times when it feels harder to connect with God. During these periods, it is crucial to persevere. Doubling down on the disciplines of prayer and Scripture, seeking encouragement from fellow believers, and reminding ourselves of God's unwavering faithfulness can help us navigate these challenging times. Remember, God's love for us does not fluctuate based on our feelings or our performance. He remains faithful, even when we falter.

The impact of this vibrant, personal relationship with God extends beyond our own spiritual well-being; it profoundly shapes the spiritual atmosphere of our homes. When our homes are built on the foundation of a genuine connection with God, His peace, His love, and His presence become palpable. Our children learn about faith not just from what we say, but from how we live, how we pray, and how we love. They witness firsthand the transformative power of a life lived in communion with the Almighty. This is the true essence of a godly home – a place where God is honored, where His Word is cherished, and where His presence is a daily reality.

To summarize, a personal relationship with God is not an optional extra for building a godly home; it is the very core. It is the source of our strength, our wisdom, and our capacity to love unconditionally. By prioritizing prayer, meditating on Scripture, and seeking moments of quiet reflection, we nurture this vital connection. By integrating spiritual disciplines into our daily lives, even in small ways, we ensure that this relationship permeates every aspect of our existence. This intimate communion empowers us to love our families with the enduring love of Christ, to face challenges with resilience, and to lead our homes with divine wisdom. It is through this deep, personal connection that our homes become true sanctuaries, reflecting the glory and grace of God in all that we do. It is a continuous, precious pursuit that underpins every other aspect of creating a family life rooted in faith.

As we've established the vital importance of cultivating a personal, intimate relationship with God, we now turn our attention to extending that spiritual vitality into the very fabric of our family life. Building a godly home is not simply about having a personal faith; it is about intentionally fostering a shared spiritual journey for our entire household. This intentionality begins with establishing clear spiritual goals for our families. Just as we might set goals for our children's education, physical health, or even extracurricular activities, we must also be purposeful in setting objectives for our family's spiritual development. This is not about imposing a rigid, joyless regimen, but rather about discerning what God desires for our unique family unit and then actively working towards those aspirations with His guidance.

The process of setting spiritual goals for your household should be deeply rooted in prayer. Before we even begin to consider specific outcomes, we must seek the heart of God for our families. What aspects of spiritual growth does He want to emphasize within our home at this particular season of life? This isn't a one-time task, but an ongoing dialogue with our Heavenly Father. We can begin by carving out dedicated time for prayer, perhaps during our quiet time, or even as a family if age appropriate. We can ask questions like: "Lord, what do You desire for our family's spiritual life? What areas do You want us to focus on growing in?" Is it a deeper appreciation for corporate worship, a more consistent practice of family devotions, or perhaps a greater emphasis on living out our faith through acts of service and kindness? God's desire is for our families to flourish in Him, and He is eager to reveal His plans to us when we sincerely seek Him.

Consider the example of a family that might feel their children are not fully engaged during Sunday worship services. Through prayer, the parents might discern a goal to foster a greater love for corporate worship. This doesn't mean forcing children to sit still or be silent; rather, it might involve praying for their hearts to be open to God's presence in the service, for the preaching to resonate with them, and for them to understand the significance of worshipping together as a community of believers. The parents might then intentionally plan activities that connect their children to the worship experience, such as discussing the sermon afterward, having them help choose worship songs, or even preparing them beforehand about the importance of the gathering. The goal here is not mere compliance, but a genuine, heartfelt engagement with God during worship.

Another avenue for setting spiritual goals could revolve around cultivating a spirit of gratitude within the home. In a culture often characterized by entitlement and discontentment, intentionally fostering gratitude is a powerful spiritual discipline. We can pray for God to open our eyes to His blessings, both big and small, and to instill a heart of thankfulness in each family member. This might translate into a goal of initiating a daily practice of sharing what each person is thankful for around the dinner table or perhaps dedicating a specific time each week to write thank-you notes to individuals who have impacted their lives positively. The aim is to shift the family's focus from what is lacking to what God has abundantly provided, cultivating a disposition that pleases Him.

Furthermore, promoting acts of kindness and service as a family can be a significant spiritual objective. God's Word calls us to love our neighbors and to be salt and light in the world. For our families, this can mean intentionally seeking opportunities to serve others. A family might set a goal to participate in a local outreach program once a month, to consistently bring meals to a family in need, or even to brainstorm ways to bless their neighbors. The discussions and preparations for these acts of service become opportunities to teach children about compassion, generosity, and the practical outworking of their faith. It's about moving faith from an abstract concept to tangible action, demonstrating the love of Christ in tangible ways. When setting these goals, it is crucial to ensure they are realistic and impactful, aligning with biblical principles. This means avoiding overly ambitious or vague objectives. Instead of a goal like "be more spiritual," a more effective goal might be "dedicate 15 minutes each evening for family prayer and Bible reading." This is measurable, achievable, and grounded in biblical practice. The goals should also be age-appropriate for the children involved. What might be a suitable spiritual goal for teenagers will differ significantly from what can be expected of toddlers. Flexibility is also key; life circumstances change, and our spiritual goals may need to adapt accordingly. The primary consideration should always be alignment with God's Word and His leading for our families.

The proactive nature of setting these goals transforms spiritual growth from an afterthought into an intentional pursuit. It provides a roadmap for our family's spiritual journey, allowing us to be more focused and deliberate in nurturing our faith together. Without a clear vision, it's easy to drift, allowing the busyness of life to overshadow the most important aspects of our family's spiritual well-being. By setting and pursuing these God-honoring goals, we are actively participating in the work God wants to do in and through our families, creating a legacy of faith that will impact generations to come. This deliberate approach ensures that the spiritual foundation we are laying is not only strong but also actively growing and developing, reflecting the vibrant life God intends for our homes. It's about building a family culture where faith is not just spoken about, but lived out, nurtured, and celebrated, ensuring that our spiritual journey is a continuous, intentional, and deeply rewarding experience for every member of the household.

Chapter 2: Nourishing the Body, Spirit, and Home

As we've explored the foundational elements of cultivating a spiritually vibrant home, it's crucial to acknowledge that our physical well-being is inextricably linked to our spiritual capacity. The way we steward our bodies directly impacts our ability to serve God, love our families, and engage fully in the life He has called us to. This understanding isn't a New Age concept; rather, it's deeply rooted in biblical principles that have been woven into the fabric of Christian life since its inception. Our physical bodies are not merely vessels to be endured until we reach eternity; they are, in fact, temples of the Holy Spirit, entrusted to us as a sacred stewardship.

The Apostle Paul, in his letter to the Corinthians, offers profound insight into this reality. He writes, "Do you not know that your bodies are temples of the Holy Spirit, who is in you, whom you have received from God? You are not your own; you were bought at a price. Therefore, honor God with your bodies" (1 Corinthians 6:19-20). This passage is a powerful declaration that our physical existence is not independent of our spiritual identity. When we accept Christ, the Holy Spirit takes residence within us. This indwelling presence elevates our physical bodies from mere biological machines to sacred dwelling places of the divine. This is a transformative perspective, shifting our understanding of health from a personal preference to a divine imperative. Honoring God with our bodies, therefore, becomes a natural outflow of our devotion and a tangible expression of our love for Him who has redeemed us. It's an act of worship, acknowledging that every aspect of our being – including our physical health – belongs to God.

This biblical mandate for physical health is not about achieving an idealized physique or adhering to a rigid set of dietary or exercise rules dictated by the culture. Instead, it's about cultivating a mindful and responsible approach to our physical well-being that enables us to live more effectively for Christ. It's about recognizing that a strong, healthy body provides us with the energy and stamina needed to fulfill our God-given responsibilities – whether that's raising children, serving in our communities, engaging in our vocations, or simply living out the Great Commission. When our bodies are neglected, weakened by poor habits, or burdened by preventable illnesses, our capacity to serve is diminished. We become less effective witnesses, less available to our families, and less able to contribute to the work of God's kingdom.

The Old Testament provides numerous examples and principles that underscore the importance of physical health. In the Law given to the Israelites, there were regulations concerning diet, hygiene, and even rest. These were not arbitrary rules but were designed to promote a healthy and vibrant community, reflecting God's desire for His people to flourish. The concept of the "Sabbath," for instance, wasn't just a day of spiritual rest but also a physical respite from labor, allowing the body and mind to recover. This emphasis on holistic well-being – encompassing physical, mental, and spiritual aspects – demonstrates that God's concern for us extends to every dimension of our lives. Consider the dietary laws in Leviticus, which, while often seen as ceremonial, also had practical implications for health in the ancient world. These guidelines encouraged responsible food choices, contributing to the overall well-being of the community.

Jesus Himself modeled a life of balance and care for His physical needs. He ate, He slept, and He sought times of solitude and rest, even amidst His demanding ministry. He understood that physical sustenance was necessary to carry out His divine mission. When He spoke of "life to the full" (John 10:10), it encompassed not only spiritual abundance but also the capacity to live vibrantly and effectively in the earthly realm. This means that prioritizing our health is not a selfish indulgence, but a practical act of obedience and a wise investment in our ability to serve. When we take care of our bodies, we are better equipped to nurture our families, to pour into our communities, and to live out the gospel with energy and enthusiasm.

The idea that prioritizing wellness is selfish stems from a misunderstanding of its purpose. If our focus is solely on self-gratification or achieving an external ideal, then it can certainly become self-centered. However, when our motivation for health is rooted in honoring God and being better equipped to serve others, it transforms into an act of worship and a ministry. Think of it this way: a mother who neglects her health might find herself too exhausted to engage with her children, too unwell to prepare nutritious meals, or too weak to participate in church activities. In contrast, a mother who prioritizes her physical well-being is better able to be present, energetic, and joyful in her family life. She has the strength to read bedtime stories, the stamina to manage a household, and the vitality to be an encouraging presence. This isn't about being perfect or never getting sick; it's about making a conscious effort to steward the body God has given us.

Furthermore, our approach to health should be one of grace, not legalism. The Bible doesn't present a detailed prescriptive diet or exercise plan for believers today in the same way it did for ancient Israel. Instead, it provides overarching principles that we can apply in wisdom and discernment. These principles encourage us to be temperate, to exercise self-control, and to make choices that are life-giving rather than destructive. It's about listening to our bodies, understanding our unique needs, and making informed decisions that honor God in our everyday habits. This might involve making conscious choices about nutrition, incorporating regular physical activity, ensuring adequate rest, and managing stress effectively.

Consider the wisdom found in Proverbs. "Do not be over-wise but fear the Lord and turn away from evil. This will bring health to your body and nourishment to your bones" (Proverbs 3:7-8). This verse connects wisdom, fear of the Lord, and turning from evil with physical health. It suggests that a life lived in accordance with God's principles is inherently conducive to well-being. This isn't a promise of immunity from illness, but a recognition that a life surrendered to God often leads to healthier choices and a greater sense of peace, which positively impacts our physical state.

As wives and mothers, we are often the primary caregivers in our homes. Our energy levels, our resilience, and our overall health directly influence the well-being of our entire family. When we are run down, it affects our patience, our ability to manage the household, and even our spiritual engagement. By intentionally prioritizing our physical health, we are essentially strengthening our capacity to nurture and lead our families in a godly manner. It's like ensuring the foundational infrastructure of a home is sound so that the entire structure can stand firm and function effectively.

The concept of stewardship extends to every resource God has given us, and our bodies are among the most precious. They are the instruments through which we interact with the world, express our love, and carry out our responsibilities. To neglect them is to neglect a gift from God, a gift that has been purchased with the precious blood of Christ. This understanding should motivate us to approach our health with a sense of reverence and responsibility. It's about seeing our bodies as tools for God's glory, and like any tool, they need to be maintained and cared for to function at their best.

This doesn't mean that every decision must be weighed against its spiritual impact. We are called to enjoy the good things God provides, including nourishing food and the simple pleasures of physical activity. The key is balance and intention. It's about moving away from a mindset of indulgence or neglect towards one of mindful stewardship. For example, choosing to prepare a wholesome meal for your family, even when you're tired, is an act of love and stewardship. Similarly, making time for a walk, even when your to-do list is overwhelming, can be a wise investment in your ability to be more productive and present later on.

The impact of our health choices extends beyond our immediate physical state. Poor health habits can lead to chronic conditions that require significant resources, time, and emotional energy, not only for ourselves but also for our families. This can detract from our ability to focus on spiritual growth and service. Conversely, a commitment to a healthy lifestyle can free up our resources and energy, allowing us to be more present and effective in all areas of our lives. It enables us to have the stamina for discipleship, the clarity of mind for prayer and biblical study, and the energy for acts of service.

In the context of family life, modeling healthy habits is also a powerful form of discipleship. Our children learn by observing us. When they see us prioritizing nutritious food, engaging in physical activity, and managing stress in healthy ways, they are more likely to adopt these practices themselves. This isn't about perfectionism, but about consistent effort and a willingness to learn and grow together as a family. It creates a family culture where well-being is valued, and were taking care of oneself is seen as a natural and important part of life.

The journey of prioritizing physical health is a continuous process of learning, adjusting, and relying on God's wisdom. It's about making incremental changes that lead to lasting habits. It's recognizing that we are not alone in this endeavor; we can pray for strength, wisdom, and self-control, and we can also seek support from our community. The goal is not to achieve perfect health, but to faithfully steward the bodies God has given us, enabling us to live lives that are full of purpose, energy, and devotion to Him. By honoring God with our physical beings, we are better equipped to nourish our spirits, strengthen our homes, and effectively shine His light in the world.

This holistic approach to wellness is a profound expression of our faith, demonstrating that our commitment to Christ permeates every aspect of our lives, including the very way we inhabit our physical bodies. It's about living a life that is not just spiritually vibrant, but also physically robust and capable of carrying out the work God has laid before us, truly embodying the concept of being a temple of the Holy Spirit.

In our pursuit of a home that nourishes the body, spirit, and soul, the kitchen often stands as the central hub of activity and a powerful expression of love. As wives and mothers, we are entrusted with the significant responsibility of feeding our families, a task that, when approached with intention and wisdom, can be a profound act of worship and a cornerstone of family well-being. This isn't about striving for culinary perfection or adhering to unattainable ideals; rather, it's about embracing practical, God-honoring strategies to create meals that are both wholesome and joyfully shared. The goal is to transform meal preparation from a potential source of stress into an opportunity for connection, nourishment, and spiritual growth, fostering a home where every bite contributes to the family's vitality.

Creating nutritious and wholesome family meals begins with a foundational understanding of what "nourishing" truly means. It encompasses not just the physical sustenance provided by food, but also the emotional and spiritual nourishment that happens around the table. In a world saturated with convenience foods and often conflicting dietary advice, it can feel overwhelming to navigate the path toward healthy eating. However, by grounding ourselves in biblical principles and practical wisdom, we can approach meal planning and preparation with confidence and creativity. The Bible itself speaks to the goodness of food and the importance of sharing meals. In Acts, the early believers "broke bread in their homes and ate together with glad and sincere hearts" (Acts 2:46). This image highlights the communal aspect of eating, where fellowship and gratitude were intertwined with the act of consumption. Our kitchens and dining tables can, and should, be extensions of this sacred practice, places where love is expressed through good food and shared moments.

One of the most impactful ways to ensure our family meals are nutritious and wholesome is to prioritize whole, unprocessed foods. This means making a conscious effort to build meals around ingredients that are as close to their natural state as possible. Think fresh fruits and vegetables bursting with vitamins and minerals, lean proteins that provide essential building blocks for the body, and whole grains that offer sustained energy and fiber. Minimizing processed foods – those that have undergone significant alteration and often contain added sugars, unhealthy fats, and artificial ingredients – is a key strategy. While occasional treats are perfectly fine, the bulk of our family's diet should consist of foods that genuinely nourish and build up. This might involve rediscovering the beauty of cooking from scratch, where we have complete control over the ingredients. It could mean embracing the seasonality of produce, seeking out local farmers' markets when possible, and making simple swaps, like choosing brown rice over white, or whole wheat pasta over refined. The effort invested in preparing meals from whole ingredients is an investment in our family's health, laying a foundation for stronger immune systems, better energy levels, and overall well-being.

Budget-friendly meal planning is also a crucial aspect of creating wholesome family meals, especially for those of us managing household finances. Healthy eating doesn't have to be expensive. In fact, by being strategic, we can often eat more healthily on a tighter budget than by relying on pre-packaged or restaurant meals. This involves smart shopping, meal planning, and minimizing food waste. Creating a weekly meal plan is perhaps the single most effective tool for both healthy eating and budget control. Before heading to the grocery store, take stock of what you already have in your pantry, refrigerator, and freezer. Then, plan your meals around those items, supplementing with necessary purchases. This approach not only reduces impulse buys and food waste but also ensures that you're buying what you need for planned meals. When grocery shopping, focus on nutrient-dense staples that offer good value, such as dried beans and lentils, oats, rice, potatoes, seasonal vegetables, and less expensive cuts of meat that can be made tender through slow cooking. Buying in bulk for non-perishables can also lead to significant savings. Learning a few simple recipes that utilize these budget-friendly ingredients can become a valuable asset in your homemaking repertoire. For instance, a hearty lentil soup, a flavorful bean chili, or a roasted chicken with root vegetables can stretch a small budget while providing a complete and nutritious meal.

Incorporating variety into our family's diet is another aspect of creating wholesome meals that caters to different tastes and ensures a broad spectrum of nutrients. Children, in particular, can sometimes be hesitant to try new foods. Patience and persistence are key. Instead of forcing them, try offering new foods alongside familiar favorites, presenting them in appealing ways, and involving them in the preparation process. When children have a hand in growing, selecting, or cooking food, they are often more inclined to try it. Experimenting with different cuisines and cooking methods can also introduce new flavors and textures, making meals more exciting. Don't be afraid to adapt recipes to suit your family's preferences. If your children dislike a particular vegetable, perhaps try a different preparation method or substitute it with a similar, more accepted vegetable. The goal is to foster an adventurous palate and a positive relationship with food, not to rigidly adhere to a prescribed menu. Remember, consistent exposure is often more effective than pressure.

Shared mealtimes are more than just opportunities to refuel our bodies; they are precious moments for connection and spiritual reflection. In our fast-paced world, it can be challenging to gather the family around the table regularly. However, the effort invested in creating these shared experiences is immeasurable. These are the times when conversations flow, laughter rings out, and family bonds are strengthened. We can use these moments to actively listen to our children's day, share our own experiences, and offer encouragement. Beyond the familial connection, mealtimes can also be a natural setting for spiritual reflection. Before the meal, we can take a moment to offer a prayer of thanks for the food, for our family, and for God's provision. We can also use this time to discuss biblical principles that relate to gratitude, stewardship, or the importance of community. Perhaps you can read a short devotional passage, share a verse of scripture, or simply talk about how God has been present in your lives that day. These small acts can weave faith into the fabric of everyday life, reminding everyone at the table of God's goodness and our dependence on Him. It transforms a simple meal into a sacred gathering, a tangible expression of our faith lived out in the home.

Turning the kitchen into a place of blessing involves more than just the food prepared within it. It's about cultivating an atmosphere of love, peace, and intentionality. When we approach our kitchens with a joyful heart and a spirit of service, that energy often permeates the food and the experience of eating it. This might involve creating a welcoming space, perhaps with a few simple decorations, a playlist of uplifting music, or even a small herb garden on the windowsill. It's about embracing the process of cooking and serving as an act of love for our families, recognizing that our efforts contribute to their physical and emotional well-being. Even on busy days, a few minutes spent tidying up before starting to cook or taking a moment to breathe and pray before embarking on meal preparation, can shift our perspective. Think of your kitchen not just as a place where food is made, but as a sanctuary where nourishment, both physical and spiritual, is cultivated. This mindset can transform the daily task of cooking into a ministry of love within your own home.

Empowering ourselves with the confidence to nourish our families well comes from a combination of knowledge, practice, and faith. It's okay to start small. If you're new to cooking or focusing on healthier options, begin with one or two new recipes a week. Gradually expand your repertoire and your comfort level. Don't be discouraged by occasional culinary mishaps; they are part of the learning process. Seek out resources that resonate with you – cookbooks, blogs, online tutorials, or even wisdom from trusted friends and family members. Perhaps there are specific cooking classes or workshops you could attend. Most importantly, remember that you are not alone in this endeavor. You can pray for wisdom, creativity, and energy in your kitchen. You can also lean on the support of your community, sharing ideas and encouragement with other women who are on a similar journey. When we approach our kitchens with a willing heart and a reliance on God's strength, we can indeed create meals that are a blessing to our families, fostering a home that is vibrant, healthy, and filled with His love. The act of nourishing our families is a powerful way we can steward the gifts God has given us, building up our households and honoring Him in the process.

As we delve deeper into the practicalities of creating these wholesome meals, let's consider the foundational elements of a well-stocked pantry and refrigerator. Having the right ingredients on hand can significantly reduce the stress associated with last-minute meal planning and encourage healthier choices. A well-organized pantry, stocked with staples, serves as the backbone of efficient meal preparation. This includes items like various types of grains (rice, quinoa, oats, whole wheat pasta), legumes (dried beans, lentils, chickpeas), healthy fats (olive oil, coconut oil, nuts, seeds), sweeteners (honey, maple syrup, dates), and flavorful seasonings (herbs, spices, vinegars). Building a good stock of these versatile ingredients allows for a wide range of meal possibilities. For instance, a bag of lentils can become a hearty soup, a flavorful side dish, or a meat substitute in tacos or shepherd's pie. Oats can be transformed into breakfast porridge, healthy cookies, or a binder for savory patties.

Beyond the pantry, a well-managed refrigerator and freezer are equally important. Fresh produce, while essential, can be more perishable. Therefore, a smart strategy involves purchasing fruits and vegetables that are in season, as they are typically more affordable and flavorful. Learning to properly store these items will extend their shelf life and minimize waste. For instance, leafy greens can be washed, dried, and stored in airtight containers with a paper towel to absorb excess moisture. Root vegetables tend to last longer when stored in a cool, dark place. Freezing is also an excellent option for preserving food and maintaining its nutritional value. Many fruits and vegetables can be blanched and frozen for later use, and leftovers from meals can be portioned and frozen for quick, convenient future meals. Think of your freezer as a personal convenience store, filled with healthy options that can be pulled out on busy days. This proactive approach to stocking and managing your kitchen ensures that you are always prepared to create a nutritious meal, even when time is short.

When it comes to minimizing processed foods, it's helpful to understand what to look for and what to avoid. Generally, the fewer ingredients listed on a food label, and the more recognizable those ingredients are, the better. Foods high in added sugars, refined grains, excessive sodium, and unhealthy trans fats should be consumed in moderation. This often means reading labels carefully and making informed choices. For example, instead of buying pre-made sauces or marinades, which can be laden with sugar and sodium, consider making your own from scratch using herbs, spices, and natural sweeteners. Similarly, instead of sugary breakfast cereals, opt for plain oatmeal topped with fresh fruit and nuts. Choosing whole, unprocessed ingredients empowers us to control the quality of the food our families consume, ensuring that we are truly nourishing them with goodness.

The art of adapting recipes to suit your family's preferences and dietary needs is a hallmark of resourceful homemaking. Children's tastes can be notoriously fickle, and sometimes what appeals to one child might not appeal to another. Instead of making multiple separate meals, which can be exhausting, try to create a "build-your-own" style meal. Tacos, for instance, can be a fantastic family favorite where each person can assemble their own with various fillings and toppings. Similarly, a baked potato bar or a pasta night with an assortment of sauces and mix-ins can cater to diverse preferences. This approach not only simplifies meal preparation but also fosters a sense of autonomy for children, allowing them to make choices within healthy parameters. If a family member has a specific dietary restriction or allergy, such as gluten intolerance or dairy sensitivity, there are countless delicious and healthy alternatives available today. Many recipes can be easily modified with gluten-free flours, dairy-free milk alternatives, or other suitable substitutes. The key is to view these adaptations not as limitations, but as opportunities for culinary creativity.

Furthermore, the practice of involving children in meal preparation, even from a young age, can instill valuable life skills and a deeper appreciation for food. Toddlers can help wash produce, stir ingredients, or set the table. Older children can learn to chop vegetables (with supervision), measure ingredients, or even follow simple recipes independently. This involvement not only frees up some of your time but also provides invaluable learning experiences. It teaches them about following instructions, understanding measurements, and the satisfaction of contributing to the family's well-being. It also demystifies the cooking process, making them more adventurous eaters and future capable cooks. Imagine the joy and pride a child feels when they serve a dish they helped create! This shared activity cultivates a sense of teamwork and family unity, strengthening the bonds around the kitchen and the dining table.

Beyond the practical aspects of nutrition and budget, fostering a positive mealtime environment is paramount. This means creating a space where conversation is encouraged, listening is practiced, and everyone feels valued. It's about making the dining table a sanctuary from the day's stresses, a place of connection and affirmation. Even on days when meals are simple or the house feels chaotic, the act of coming together to share food is significant. Minimizing distractions, such as screens, during mealtimes can greatly enhance this connection. Instead, encourage eye contact, active listening, and sharing about one's day. These shared moments, filled with both spoken and unspoken love, are deeply nourishing to the soul.

The spiritual dimension of shared meals can be intentionally cultivated. As mentioned earlier, a prayer of gratitude before eating is a beautiful practice. However, this can extend beyond a simple blessing. You might use mealtimes to discuss how the food itself reflects God's creation and provision. For example, when eating fruits or vegetables, you could talk about the miracle of growth, the sun, and the rain that contributed to their existence. Sharing a verse that speaks to gratitude, hospitality, or fellowship can also be meaningful. Even a simple conversation about how you saw God's hand at work during the day can foster a sense of shared faith and dependence on Him. These intentional moments, woven into the fabric of daily life, can help children develop a robust faith that is integrated into all aspects of their lives, including the simple act of eating together.

Ultimately, creating nutritious and wholesome family meals is a journey, not a destination. It's about progress, not perfection. There will be days when meals are less than ideal, and that is perfectly fine. The key is to embrace the process with grace, learn from each experience, and consistently strive to honor God with the way we care for our families. By equipping ourselves with practical knowledge, planning with intention, and approaching our kitchens with a spirit of love and gratitude, we can transform meal preparation into a joyful expression of our faith and a powerful way to nourish our families, body, spirit, and soul. The kitchen becomes more than just a place where food is made; it becomes a sanctuary of love, a hub of connection, and a cornerstone of a thriving, God-honoring home. It's in these daily acts of service, infused with faith and love, that we truly build a life that pleases Him.

The demands of homemaking, particularly for a wife and mother, are vast and multifaceted. We are tasked with nurturing our families' physical needs through meals, maintaining a clean and orderly home, managing schedules, and often, contributing to the family's income or emotional well-being in significant ways. In the midst of this constant giving, it is incredibly easy for our own well-being to be relegated to the bottom of the priority list. We may even feel a sense of guilt for prioritizing our own needs, viewing it as selfish or a sign of weakness. However, as we are called to be good stewards of all that God has entrusted to us, this includes the stewardship of our own bodies, minds, and spirits. True self-care, viewed through a biblical lens, is not about indulgence or selfishness; it is about essential spiritual and physical maintenance that enables us to serve more effectively and to reflect God's love more fully.

When we consider self-care from a Christian perspective, it's important to define it not as an escape from our responsibilities, but as a strategic and intentional investment in our capacity to fulfill them. The Bible speaks extensively about the importance of rest and renewal. In the creation account, God Himself rested on the seventh day (Genesis 2:2-3), setting a divine pattern for humanity. Jesus, despite His demanding ministry, frequently sought out solitude and rest: "Come with me by yourselves to a quiet place and get some rest" (Mark 6:31). This demonstrates that even the Son of God recognized the necessity of taking time for personal replenishment. Furthermore, the Apostle Paul encouraged believers to take care of themselves, stating, "Or do you not know that your body is a temple of the Holy Spirit within you, whom you have from God? You are not your own, for you have been bought with a price: therefore glorify God in your body" (1 Corinthians 6:19-20). This verse powerfully underscores that our physical and mental well-being are not merely personal matters, but are integral to honoring God.

Therefore, self-care for the homemaker is about actively engaging in practices that restore and refresh us, enabling us to operate from a place of abundance rather than depletion. It's about recognizing that we cannot pour from an empty cup. When we are constantly giving without receiving, our energy wanes, our patience frays, and our ability to engage joyfully in our roles diminishes. This can lead to burnout, resentment, and a diminished capacity to be the nurturing presence our families need. By intentionally carving out time for personal restoration, we are actually strengthening our ability to serve, enhancing our resilience, and modeling a healthy approach to life for our children. It is a vital aspect of effective stewardship, ensuring that the resources God has given us – our energy, our emotional capacity, our physical health – are maintained and optimized.

One of the most foundational aspects of self-care is adequate rest. In our culture, sleep is often seen as a luxury rather than a necessity. We may find ourselves sacrificing sleep to get more done, believing that the extra hour of productivity is worth the cost. However, chronic sleep deprivation has significant negative impacts on our physical health, cognitive function, emotional regulation, and spiritual vitality. When we are well-rested, we are more patient, more creative, have better focus, and are less prone to irritability and anxiety. Prioritizing sleep might involve establishing a consistent bedtime routine, creating a restful sleep environment, and being disciplined about winding down before bed. This could mean putting away screens an hour before sleep, enjoying a warm bath, reading a comforting book, or engaging in quiet prayer. It's about creating the conditions for our bodies and minds to truly rest and repair. For homemakers, this often requires a conscious effort to delegate tasks, say no to non-essential commitments, and perhaps even communicate needs to family members so that expectations are realistic regarding our energy levels. It's about recognizing that a well-rested mother is a more effective and joyful mother.

Beyond physical rest, spiritual rejuvenation is equally crucial. This involves intentionally nurturing our relationship with God. For many, this looks like dedicated quiet time each day – a time set aside for prayer, reading Scripture, meditation, and listening for God's voice. This isn't about adding another item to a to-do list, but about connecting with the source of our strength and purpose. Even a short period of focused spiritual engagement can profoundly shift our perspective and renew our spirit. Perhaps it's reading a Psalm and praying through it, journaling about your walk with God, or simply sitting in His presence in silence. It might be listening to worship music while you fold laundry or taking a walk in nature and reflecting on God's creation. The key is regularity and intentionality. When our spiritual well is replenished, we are better equipped to handle the emotional and mental demands of homemaking. This consistent connection reminds us of our identity in Christ, reinforces our purpose, and allows us to approach our duties with a renewed sense of joy and grace.

Furthermore, engaging in activities that bring us personal joy and fulfillment, often referred to as hobbies or personal interests, can be a powerful form of self-care. These are activities that we genuinely enjoy and that allow us to express our creativity, learn new skills, or simply de-stress. For one homemaker, this might be gardening, for another it could be painting, knitting, baking for pleasure, writing, playing a musical instrument, or engaging in physical activity like yoga or swimming. These activities are not frivolous; they are essential for maintaining a sense of self beyond our roles as wife and mother. They provide an outlet for creativity and personal expression, which can be deeply fulfilling. Finding even small pockets of time to engage in these passions can make a significant difference in our overall well-being. It's about carving out moments to nurture the parts of ourselves that are distinct from our domestic responsibilities, reminding us that we are multifaceted individuals with unique gifts and interests.

It is also important to acknowledge the value of social connection as a component of self-care. While our primary focus is often our immediate family, healthy relationships with other adults are vital for our emotional and mental health. This might involve nurturing friendships with other women who understand the unique challenges and joys of homemaking and motherhood. Having a supportive community can provide encouragement, practical advice, and a sense of belonging. Regular calls with a friend, a coffee date, or participation in a women's Bible study can be incredibly refreshing. These interactions offer a chance to share burdens, celebrate joys, and receive perspective from those who are walking a similar path. It's a reminder that we are not alone in our endeavors and that community is a God-given resource for strength and support. Practical implementation of self-care requires intentionality and strategic planning within the context of a busy life. It's not about waiting for free time to magically appear, but about actively creating it. This might involve a conversation with your spouse about sharing household responsibilities or delegating certain tasks to older children. It could mean setting boundaries with external commitments that drain your energy without offering reciprocal value. For example, if you find yourself overextended with volunteer work that leaves you feeling depleted, it might be time to re-evaluate those commitments. Sometimes, self-care looks like saying "no" to things that are not essential, freeing up time and energy for what truly matters. It also involves learning to be efficient in our daily tasks, so that we can create more breathing room. This could mean meal prepping on the weekend, establishing morning or evening routines that streamline household chores, or decluttering our homes to reduce the time spent on upkeep. The goal is to create a rhythm that supports our well-being, not one that constantly drains us.

It's also essential to remember that self-care is not a one-size-fits-all approach. What is restorative and life-giving for one person might not be for another. The key is to prayerfully discern what truly nourishes your soul, body, and mind. This might involve a period of experimentation and reflection. For some, it might be as simple as a quiet cup of tea on the porch for ten minutes each morning. For others, it could be a longer block of time, like a weekly walk in the park or a monthly outing with friends. It's about identifying the practices that leave you feeling more energized, more peaceful, and more equipped to face the day's challenges, all while honoring God in the process.

We must also address the potential for guilt that often accompanies the idea of self-care for homemakers. In a society that often glorifies busyness and sacrifice, taking time for oneself can feel counterintuitive or even selfish. However, this perspective is not rooted in biblical wisdom. God designed us with needs for rest, replenishment, and connection. Honoring those needs is not selfish; it is responsible stewardship. When we neglect our own well-being, we are less effective in all areas of our lives. Our capacity for love, patience, and joy diminishes, which ultimately impacts our families negatively. Therefore, viewing self-care as a vital component of our calling as wives and mothers allows us to approach it with a clear conscience, knowing that it is an investment in our ability to serve and to reflect Christ's love. It's about recognizing that our worth is not solely defined by our productivity or our ability to constantly serve others without replenishing ourselves. Our worth is found in Christ, and caring for the temple He has given us is a way of honoring Him.

Moreover, self-care is not a destination but an ongoing practice. Life is dynamic, and our needs will change. What is restorative today might not be what we need next month or next year. It requires ongoing awareness and a willingness to adapt our self-care strategies as our circumstances evolve. A season of young children will require different approaches to self-care than a season with teenagers or when children have left the home. It is a commitment to listen to our bodies, our minds, and our spirits, and to respond with grace and wisdom. This might mean revisiting our quiet time practices, adjusting our sleep schedules, or seeking out new forms of rejuvenation. The important thing is to remain committed to the principle of self-stewardship as a means of honoring God and serving our families well.

Ultimately, embracing self-care as a Christian homemaker is a profound act of faith and obedience. It is acknowledging that we are finite beings who are sustained by an infinite God. By intentionally seeking rest, spiritual renewal, personal joy, and community, we are better equipped to carry out the beautiful and vital work of nurturing our homes and families. It allows us to be more present, more patient, more joyful, and more resilient. It transforms us from simply managing a household to actively cultivating a life that honors God in every aspect, including the stewardship of our own well-being. When we are replenished, our capacity to pour love, grace, and life into our homes is magnified, creating a more vibrant and God-honoring environment for all. This commitment to self-care is not a detour from our calling; it is an essential part of fulfilling it with excellence and enduring joy. It allows us to approach each day, each task, and each family member from a place of strength and abundance, reflecting the very abundance of God's provision for us.

Establishing Healthy Fitness Routines

In the whirlwind of homemaking, where demands on our time and energy seem endless, the idea of incorporating a fitness routine can feel like another insurmountable task. We often picture grueling gym sessions or lengthy runs, scenarios that seem utterly incompatible with the realities of managing a household, nurturing young children, or balancing multiple responsibilities. However, the truth is that a healthy fitness routine doesn't require a complete overhaul of our lives or vast amounts of free time. Instead, it's about finding practical, sustainable ways to move our bodies that fit into the rhythm of our days, ultimately enhancing our capacity to serve and to thrive. Viewing physical activity not as a chore, but as a vital act of stewardship for the bodies God has given us, can transform our perspective and motivation. As we are called to honor God with our bodies, which are temples of the Holy Spirit, this extends to caring for them through regular movement.

The benefits of physical activity extend far beyond the aesthetic or the purely physical. For us as homemakers, consistent movement can be a powerful tool for managing stress, a constant companion for many in our roles. The release of endorphins during exercise acts as a natural mood elevator, helping to combat feelings of overwhelm and anxiety. When we engage in physical activity, even for short durations, we can experience increased mental clarity and focus. This renewed mental acuity is invaluable when tackling complex family schedules, problem-solving household challenges, or simply engaging with our children in a present and attentive way. Furthermore, a body that is regularly exercised is a body that has more sustained energy. Instead of feeling depleted by the end of the day, we can find ourselves with greater vitality to engage with our families and pursue our interests. This isn't about achieving a certain physique but about cultivating a resilient and energetic vessel that allows us to live more fully and serve more effectively.

Incorporating fitness into a busy family life often necessitates a shift in mindset from "no time" to "finding time" through creative integration. This might mean embracing short bursts of activity throughout the day rather than seeking out a dedicated hour-long block. For instance, utilizing transition times can be incredibly effective. While dinner is simmering or laundry is in the wash cycle, these moments can be used for a quick set of squats, lunges, or jumping jacks. Even five to ten minutes of focused movement can make a difference. Consider creating a mini-workout playlist that can be played during these intervals, making the activity more engaging. Alternatively, you can incorporate movement into your household chores. Speeding up your vacuuming, doing calf raises while waiting for water to boil, or doing a few push-ups against the kitchen counter can all add up. These small, consistent actions build momentum and reinforce the idea that fitness can be woven into the fabric of everyday life, rather than being an external imposition.

One of the most accessible and beneficial forms of exercise is walking. It requires no special equipment and can be adapted to various fitness levels. For families, making walks a regular occurrence can serve a dual purpose: promoting individual fitness and fostering family connection. Scheduling a family walk after dinner, on a Saturday morning, or as a way to unwind on a Sunday afternoon provides a structured opportunity for everyone to get moving together. These walks can be opportunities for conversation, for observing God's creation, or simply for enjoying each other's company in a relaxed setting. Even if your neighborhood isn't ideal for long walks, a brisk walk around the block, a loop through a local park, or even walking laps in your backyard can be beneficial. The key is consistency. Aim for a certain number of steps per day or a set number of walks per week, gradually increasing the duration or intensity as you feel able. Remember, the goal is progress, not perfection.

For those who prefer or require exercising at home, there are numerous resources available that require minimal space and equipment. Many online platforms offer a vast array of free workout videos, from gentle yoga and Pilates to high-intensity interval training (HIIT) and strength-building routines. You can find programs specifically designed for busy moms, targeting core strength, flexibility, or overall cardiovascular health. These can often be done in short, manageable sessions – 15 to 30 minutes can be highly effective. Consider investing in a few basic pieces of equipment like resistance bands, dumbbells, or a yoga mat, which can expand your exercise options significantly and are relatively inexpensive. The convenience of a home-based routine means no travel time, no waiting for equipment, and the ability to exercise at a time that suits you best, whether that's before the family wakes up, during nap time, or after everyone has gone to bed.

When building a fitness routine, it's important to approach it with a spirit of intentionality and to set realistic expectations. Rather than aiming for an ambitious goal that might lead to discouragement, start small. Perhaps your initial goal is to incorporate 15 minutes of movement three times a week. As you build consistency and confidence, you can gradually increase the duration, frequency, or intensity of your workouts. Listen to your body. Some days you may feel more energetic and capable of a more strenuous workout, while other days a gentle stretching routine or a leisurely walk might be more appropriate. This mindful approach prevents burnout and ensures that your fitness routine remains enjoyable and sustainable in the long term.

The spiritual benefits of physical activity are often overlooked but are profound. As mentioned, the release of endorphins can improve mood and reduce stress, creating a more peaceful internal environment. This can enhance our ability to pray, to meditate on Scripture, and to connect with God. When our bodies feel good, our minds are clearer, and our spirits are more open to spiritual input. Engaging in physical activity can also be a form of worship in itself. By caring for the physical vessel that God has entrusted to us, we are honoring Him. The discipline and perseverance required to maintain a fitness routine can also build character, teaching us patience, resilience, and self-control – virtues that are invaluable in all aspects of our lives, especially within the home. When we feel physically stronger and more energetic, our ability to engage with our families, to manage the demands of the home, and to serve others with joy and grace is significantly enhanced.

Furthermore, it is crucial to remember that consistency trumps intensity. A moderate workout done regularly is far more beneficial than sporadic, intense bursts of activity that lead to injury or burnout. Building a habit takes time, and there will be days when motivation wanes. On those days, relying on discipline rather than just emotion is key. Remind yourself of your "why" – the desire to be healthy, energetic, and to honor God with your body. It can be helpful to track your progress, whether that's through a fitness app, a journal, or simply by noting down the days you exercised. Seeing your consistency over time can be a powerful motivator.

For mothers of young children, finding personal time for exercise can be a particular challenge. However, even in these demanding seasons, movement is still possible. Consider incorporating your children into your routine. Dancing with them to music, going for a stroller walk, or doing simple exercises like lunges or crunches while they play nearby can be effective ways to get moving. There are also many mommy-and-me workout videos available online that allow you to exercise with your child. The key is adaptability and a willingness to be flexible. Sometimes, your workout might look different from what you envisioned, but the act of moving your body and prioritizing your health is what truly matters.

As we cultivate these healthy fitness routines, we are not just investing in our physical health; we are investing in our overall capacity to live a vibrant, joyful, and God-honoring life. We are equipping ourselves with the strength, energy, and mental clarity needed to nurture our homes and families effectively. This isn't about striving for perfection or comparing ourselves to others, but about a commitment to well-being as an integral part of our calling. By prioritizing movement, we honor the incredible gift of our bodies and enhance our ability to pour out love and grace from a place of abundance, not depletion. This proactive approach to our physical health is a powerful testament to our faith and a practical way to live out the biblical principle of good stewardship. The strength and resilience we build through consistent physical activity will undoubtedly ripple through every aspect of our lives, enabling us to better serve our families and to reflect the vitality and joy of Christ.

The state of our physical surroundings profoundly influences our inner landscape. Just as we strive to nourish our bodies and spirits through dedicated routines, so too must we consider the environment in which we live, work, and love. A well-ordered home is not merely an aesthetic preference; it is a foundational element that supports mental clarity, emotional stability, and spiritual peace. It provides a sanctuary from the external world, a place where our families can rest, connect, and grow. When our homes are cluttered, chaotic, or unclean, these very qualities can seep into our minds, creating a sense of overwhelm, anxiety, and a general lack of focus. Conversely, a clean, organized, and well-maintained home acts as a calming balm, reducing stress and fostering an atmosphere of tranquility. This intentionality in our homemaking reflects a deeper truth: that we are called to be stewards of the spaces God has entrusted to us, reflecting His love for order and beauty in all that we do.

The journey to a well-ordered home environment often begins with the daunting task of decluttering. In our modern world, it is so easy for possessions to accumulate, often without us even realizing the extent of it. These physical accumulations can weigh us down, not just in terms of space, but also in terms of mental energy. Every item that is out of place, every surface covered in unnecessary objects, requires a bit of our cognitive load to navigate. It's like having a constant hum of low-level distraction in the background of our lives. Decluttering is therefore an act of liberation, freeing up not only physical space but also mental bandwidth. As we begin to sort through our belongings, we can approach it with a prayerful heart, asking for wisdom and discernment. What truly serves our family's needs? What brings joy or serves a purpose? What has become a burden or a distraction? It can be helpful to tackle decluttering in small, manageable zones. Instead of attempting to declutter the entire house in one weekend, focus on a single drawer, a shelf, or a small closet. This prevents overwhelm and allows for a sense of accomplishment as you progress. The process might involve categories like "Keep," "Donate," "Discard," and perhaps a "Relocate" pile for items that belong elsewhere in the home. As we make these decisions, we are not just organizing objects; we are making conscious choices about what we allow to occupy our physical and mental space. We are actively curating an environment that supports peace and productivity. The spiritual aspect of decluttering can be particularly profound. Letting go of sentimental items that no longer serve a purpose, or items that are kept out of obligation or guilt, can be a metaphor for releasing those things in our lives that no longer align with God's will or that hold us back from spiritual growth. It's about making space for the new, for clarity, and for a lighter, more purposeful existence.

Once the initial decluttering has been addressed, establishing simple, consistent cleaning routines becomes the next vital step in maintaining an ordered home. The goal here is not to achieve a state of sterile perfection, but rather to create a sustainable rhythm of care that keeps our homes functional, healthy, and pleasant. Many of us have probably experienced the cycle of intense cleaning followed by a gradual slide back into disorder. The key to breaking this cycle lies in consistency and in embracing routines that are realistic for our season of life. Instead of thinking about cleaning as a massive undertaking to be done only occasionally, we can break it down into daily, weekly, and monthly tasks. Daily habits might include making beds, wiping down kitchen counters after meals, and a quick tidy-up of living areas before bed. These small acts, performed consistently, prevent major build-up and create a noticeable difference in the overall atmosphere of the home. Weekly routines could involve more thorough tasks such as vacuuming or mopping floors, cleaning bathrooms, changing bed linens, and dusting. It can be helpful to assign specific cleaning tasks to particular days of the week to create a predictable schedule. For instance, Mondays could be for bathrooms, Tuesdays for floors, and so on. This approach avoids the feeling of being constantly behind and ensures that essential cleaning is regularly addressed. Monthly or seasonal tasks might include things like cleaning out the refrigerator, washing windows, or deep cleaning the oven. Spreading these larger tasks out over the month or year makes them far less daunting. The beauty of these routines is that they become habits, requiring less conscious effort over time. They contribute to a sense of calm because we know that the basic maintenance of our home is being handled.

Involving the entire family in the process of maintaining order is crucial for both the effectiveness of the routines and for fostering a sense of shared responsibility and pride in the home. When children are young, their participation might be limited to simple tasks like putting away their toys, helping to set the table, or placing their dirty clothes in the hamper. As they grow older, their responsibilities can expand to include tasks such as vacuuming their own rooms, helping with laundry, or assisting with meal preparation and clean-up. It is important to approach this with patience and a willingness to teach. Children will not inherently know how to fold a shirt perfectly or how to clean a sink without instruction. Taking the time to demonstrate and to offer gentle guidance is an investment that pays dividends. We can frame these tasks not as chores, but as contributing to the family team and caring for our shared home, which is a gift from God. Creating age-appropriate chore charts can be a helpful visual aid. It provides clarity on expectations and allows children to see their contributions. Celebrating their efforts and acknowledging their help reinforces the positive behavior and encourages continued participation. Even teenagers, who may sometimes resist family involvement, can be encouraged to take ownership of certain areas or tasks. This not only eases the burden on parents but also teaches valuable life skills and promotes a sense of contribution and belonging within the family unit. The act of working together to maintain a beautiful and functional living space can also be a powerful way to build family cohesion and create lasting memories.

A well-kept home environment directly contributes to reduced stress and a more restful atmosphere for family life. When we walk into a home that is tidy, clean, and free from the visual noise of clutter, our nervous systems can actually relax. The constant background chatter of "things to do" or "things to put away" is silenced, allowing for greater peace. This is particularly important for mothers who often carry the emotional and physical weight of managing a household. A sense of order can translate into a feeling of control and competence, which are powerful antidotes to stress and overwhelm. Furthermore, a restful atmosphere is essential for effective family life. Children need a calm and predictable environment in which to decompress after school or to focus on homework. Spouses need a peaceful space to connect and to recharge. When the home is a source of stress rather than a sanctuary, it can strain relationships and diminish overall well-being. The deliberate act of creating and maintaining order is, therefore, an act of love for our families. It is a way of saying, "This is a place where you are safe, loved, and cared for." It fosters a sense of calm and well-being that permeates every interaction and activity within the home.

The principles of a well-ordered home can also be seen as an expression of our faith. The Bible speaks of God's desire for order, from the creation account to the instructions for the Tabernacle. While our homes will never be perfectly pristine, striving for orderliness reflects a reverence for the sanctity of the home and for the responsibilities God has given us as homemakers. It's about tending to the gifts we've been given with care and diligence. This intentionality can transform mundane tasks into acts of worship. When we wipe down a surface, we can do so with a prayer of gratitude for the provision that allows us to have that surface, or with a prayer for the family members who will use it. When we fold laundry, we can do so with a prayer for the person who will wear those clothes. This shift in perspective elevates the work of homemaking from a burden to a calling, a way of honoring God in the everyday. It also teaches our children invaluable lessons about stewardship, responsibility, and the beauty that comes from care and attention. They learn that their environment is something to be cherished and maintained, not neglected.

Consider the impact of a clean and organized kitchen. This is often the heart of the home, where meals are prepared, and families gather. A kitchen free from dirty dishes, sticky countertops, and overflowing bins is not only more hygienic but also more conducive to the joyful preparation of food. It invites creativity and makes the process of cooking less of a chore and more of an opportunity for nourishment and connection. Similarly, a living room that is tidy and welcoming encourages conversation and relaxation. When the main living spaces are cluttered, it can subtly discourage family members from gathering there, leading to isolation even within the same house. The same applies to bedrooms; a peaceful and organized sleeping space is essential for rest and rejuvenation, which are critical for our physical and mental health. Even seemingly small areas, like entryways or hallways, benefit from order. A clutter-free entryway creates a more pleasant transition into and out of the home, setting a positive tone from the moment one steps inside.

The process of decluttering and organizing can also be a journey of self-discovery. As we handle our possessions, we often encounter items that bring back memories, both happy and sad. This can be an opportunity to process emotions and to release any baggage that we may be carrying. Letting go of items that are no longer serving us can be a powerful act of self-care and a step towards emotional freedom. It can be helpful to have a designated spot for sentimental items that you wish to keep, perhaps a memory box or a specific shelf, so that they are cherished without contributing to overall clutter. This intentionality ensures that these precious mementos are honored while maintaining the order of the wider living space.

Establishing a cleaning schedule does not need to be rigid or complex. For many busy families, a simple system that is flexible and adaptable is the most effective. Some people find it helpful to implement a "one-in, one-out" rule for new purchases, especially for items like clothing or books, to prevent accumulation. Others find that dedicating 15-20 minutes each day to a specific "power tidy" session can make a significant difference. This might involve clearing off surfaces, sweeping a high-traffic area, or doing a quick bathroom wipe-down. The key is to find what works for your family and your unique circumstances. Remember that consistency is more important than perfection. There will be days when life happens, and the cleaning routine might be interrupted. The important thing is to get back on track as soon as possible without guilt or self-condemnation. The aim is progress, not an unattainable ideal.

Involving children in household chores from an early age instills in them a sense of responsibility, competence, and an understanding that contributing to the family unit is an important part of life. When children are taught that a well-ordered home is a reflection of a loving and functional family, they are more likely to embrace their roles. It's about more than just getting tasks done; it's about building character. Learning to follow instructions, to complete a task thoroughly, and to take pride in their contribution are all invaluable life lessons. Furthermore, as children participate in maintaining the home, they develop a greater appreciation for the effort involved and are less likely to be careless or disrespectful of their surroundings. This shared effort can also be a wonderful opportunity for connection. While folding laundry together or tidying up after dinner, conversations can flow naturally, strengthening bonds and fostering communication.

Ultimately, creating and maintaining a well-ordered home environment is an ongoing process, a journey rather than a destination. It requires intentionality, consistent effort, and a willingness to adapt as our family's needs and circumstances change. By prioritizing order and cleanliness, we are not just creating a pleasant living space; we are cultivating an atmosphere that nurtures the body, the spirit, and the relationships within our homes. We are reflecting God's beautiful design for order and care, and in doing so, we bring peace and rest to ourselves and to those we love most. This intentional focus on our home environment serves as a tangible expression of God's love, making our homes true sanctuaries where His peace can reign. The peace we cultivate within our homes can extend outwards, impacting our communities and reflecting God's goodness in a world that often feels chaotic.

Chapter 3: Cultivating a Flourishing Marriage

The covenant of marriage, as ordained by God, is a sacred union designed for companionship, procreation, and a profound reflection of Christ's love for His Church. This divine blueprint is not a rigid set of rules but rather a relational framework built on principles of sacrificial love, mutual respect, and unwavering commitment. When we approach our marriages with an understanding of this biblical foundation, we lay the groundwork for a unity that is both deeply personal and eternally significant.

Central to the biblical understanding of marriage is the concept of partnership. Genesis 2:18 tells us, "It is not good for the man to be alone. I will make a helper suitable for him." This declaration from God Himself highlights the inherent need for companionship and the complementary nature of husband and wife. The Hebrew word for "helper" (ezer) is often translated as "aid" or "support," and it carries connotations of strength and divine assistance. This isn't a one-sided dependency, but rather a mutual reliance where each spouse brings unique strengths and perspectives to the union. The creation narrative, where Eve is formed from Adam's very rib, signifies an intrinsic connection and oneness. They are two individuals, yet in marriage, they become "one flesh" (Genesis 2:24). This concept of oneness is not about the annihilation of individual identities but about a profound spiritual, emotional, and physical merging that creates a new entity – the married couple. This "one flesh" union is the bedrock of marital unity, suggesting a deep intimacy and shared destiny that transcends mere coexistence. It implies a shared life, shared resources, and shared responsibility for building a life together. This oneness is a dynamic reality that needs to be continually cultivated and nurtured throughout the marriage.

The Apostle Paul further elaborates on this marital unity and the distinct, yet complementary, roles within it in his letter to the Ephesians (Ephesians 5:22-33). He presents a Christ-centered model for marriage, calling wives to submit to their husbands as to the

Lord, and husbands to love their wives sacrificially, just as Christ loved the Church and gave Himself up for her. This is not a call for subjugation or an endorsement of any form of abuse, but a divine model of Christ-like leadership and devoted love. The husband's leadership is to be characterized by a selfless love that prioritizes his wife's well-being above his own, mirroring Christ's ultimate sacrifice. This love is not merely an emotion; it is an active, volitional choice to serve, protect, and cherish one's spouse. It requires humility, patience, and a willingness to lay down one's own desires for the good of the other. Similarly, the wife's submission is an act of reverence and respect for her husband's God-given leadership within the home, a response to his loving leadership. It is a willing yielding that strengthens the partnership and fosters a harmonious environment. This mutual submission and sacrificial love are the cornerstones of a flourishing marriage, creating a dynamic that allows both individuals to thrive within the covenant.

The covenantal aspect of marriage cannot be overstated. Unlike a contract, which can be broken or renegotiated, a covenant is a solemn promise, a binding agreement made before God. In the Old Testament, covenants were often sealed with rituals and pronouncements, signifying their enduring nature. Marriage, in the biblical sense, is similarly a covenant before God, an unbreakable bond that signifies God's faithfulness and commitment. This understanding transforms marriage from a mere human arrangement into a sacred trust, a reflection of God's own covenantal relationship with His people. Malachi 2:14 speaks of marriage as a covenant that God witnesses: "The Lord has been the witness between you and the wife of your youth, because you have been unfaithful to her, though she is your partner and your wife by covenant." This passage emphasizes that God is not a passive observer but an active participant and witness to the marital covenant. Therefore, the vows exchanged at the altar are not simply words but promises made before the Almighty, carrying profound weight and accountability. This covenantal commitment provides a secure foundation upon which the marriage can weather storms and grow stronger over time. It is a promise to stay committed through thick and thin, through joy and sorrow, through health and sickness.

This biblical framework for marital unity calls for intentional effort in cultivating love, respect, and understanding. It begins with a deep appreciation for the unique individual God has placed alongside us. Each spouse is a creation of God, with their own gifts, talents, and perspectives. Honoring these differences, rather than trying to mold the other into our own image, is crucial. When we truly see and value our spouse as God sees them, we create an environment of acceptance and affirmation. This appreciation fosters open communication, where both partners feel safe to express their thoughts, feelings, and needs without fear of judgment or rejection. Active listening, characterized by genuine interest and a desire to understand, is a vital component of this process. It means putting aside distractions, making eye contact, and responding with empathy and thoughtfulness.

Beyond communication, the biblical mandate for love in marriage is often described with the Greek word "agape." This is a selfless, unconditional, and sacrificial love that seeks the highest good of the beloved. It is not dependent on feelings or circumstances, but on a deliberate choice to act in ways that benefit and honor the spouse. This kind of love is cultivated through acts of kindness, words of encouragement, and a consistent effort to prioritize the other's needs. It means forgiving freely, offering grace, and extending compassion, just as Christ has forgiven and shown grace to us. This forgiveness is not about condoning wrongdoing but about releasing resentment and choosing to move forward in love. It is a powerful force that can heal wounds and strengthen the marital bond.

The concept of shared purpose further solidifies marital unity. When a couple aligns their lives around shared values and goals, and ultimately, around serving God together, their bond is strengthened.

This doesn't mean they will agree on every single issue, but rather that they have a common direction and a shared vision for their life together. This might involve raising children with godly principles, serving in ministry, or pursuing common interests that bring them closer. When a couple operates as a team, with each member contributing their unique strengths towards a common objective, they experience a sense of fulfillment and accomplishment that is greater than anything they could achieve individually. This shared journey towards fulfilling God's purpose for their lives becomes a powerful testament to their unity.

The spiritual dimension of this unity is perhaps the most profound. When both husband and wife are committed to growing in their faith and pursuing God together, their marriage becomes a spiritual partnership. They can pray together, study scripture together, and encourage each other in their walk with the Lord. This shared spiritual journey creates an unshakeable foundation, anchoring their marriage in something far greater than themselves. It provides a source of strength during difficult times and a constant reminder of the eternal purpose for their union. The marital relationship becomes a living testament to Christ's love for the Church, a visible manifestation of God's grace and faithfulness in the world. This spiritual intimacy fosters a depth of connection that transcends the physical and emotional, creating a bond that is truly unbreakable.

The biblical blueprint for marital unity is a call to an active, ongoing process of building and strengthening the relationship. It is not a passive state but a dynamic engagement with one another, rooted in God's unchanging love and faithfulness. By embracing these principles, couples can cultivate marriages that not only flourish in the present but also stand as enduring testaments to God's design for love, companionship, and covenant. It requires a commitment to see marriage not as a destination but as a journey, where each day presents an opportunity to deepen intimacy, foster respect, and reflect the love of Christ. This intentionality in building marital unity is a sacred trust, a vital aspect of honoring God and building a lasting legacy of love. The strength of this unity is often tested, but the biblical principles provide a timeless guide to navigate those challenges and emerge even stronger, a reflection of the enduring love between Christ and His Church.

The rhythm of a household, particularly one filled with the joyful chaos of children and the daily necessities of managing a home, can easily become a relentless cycle that leaves little room for the core relationship it's built upon the marriage itself. It is so easy, so natural even, for the roles of mother and homemaker to absorb our entire identity, pushing our partnership with our husband to the periphery. Yet, the very foundation of our family's well-being rests on the strength and health of this primary relationship. Prioritizing your husband isn't a selfish act; it's a foundational act of love and stewardship for your entire family. When we intentionally carve out space and cultivate connection with our husbands, we are not neglecting our other duties but rather reinforcing the very structure that supports them.

The demands on a wife and mother are multifaceted and often all-consuming. From the early morning wake-up calls to the late-night bedtime routines, from meal preparation and cleaning to managing schedules and nurturing little hearts, the days can feel like a blur of activity. In this constant state of giving, it's incredibly easy for personal needs and the needs of our spouse to get pushed aside. We might find ourselves operating on autopilot, our conversations reduced to logistical updates about children's activities or household chores. This is a dangerous path, one that can lead to a slow, silent drifting apart, where intimacy erodes and the bond that once felt unbreakable begins to fray. The biblical call to "leave and cleave" (Genesis 2:24) signifies the creation of a new, primary unit, and while the demands of family life are sacred, they should not eclipse the importance of that initial, foundational covenant. Therefore, making intentional efforts to prioritize your husband, to nurture your connection, is not just beneficial; it is essential for the flourishing of your marriage and, by extension, your entire family.

One of the most effective ways to prioritize your husband is through the deliberate creation of quality time. In the busyness of life, this often requires a conscious and consistent effort. Date nights, whether once a week or once a month, are a crucial opportunity to reconnect outside the context of daily responsibilities. These are not just for frivolous enjoyment; they are sacred spaces for communication, for rekindling romance, and for remembering why you fell in love in the first place. Plan something that allows for uninterrupted conversation, where you can truly see and hear each other. This might mean arranging for a babysitter and going out to a favorite restaurant, or it could be a more creative approach at home. A "dinner and a movie" night after the children are asleep, with a special meal prepared and a deliberate effort made to engage with each other, can be just as effective. The key is the intention behind it: setting aside the distractions of the world and focusing solely on each other.

Beyond dedicated date nights, daily intentionality is equally, if not more, vital. These small, consistent acts of connection can build a powerful reservoir of intimacy that sustains the marriage through tougher times. Consider establishing a routine of a brief, focused check-in each day. This might be the first thing you do after the children have gone to school, or it could be a few minutes before bed. The purpose is to engage in genuine conversation, not just to exchange information. Ask your husband about his day, not just what happened, but how he felt about it, what challenged him, what brought him joy. Listen actively, with your full attention. Put down your phone, turn off the television, and make eye contact. Share your own experiences, your thoughts, and your feelings. These moments, though brief, communicate that he is seen, heard, and valued, even amidst the surrounding demands.

Moreover, cultivate ways to express love and appreciation that are specific to your husband. Consider his "love language" as described by Gary Chapman. Is he someone who thrives on words of affirmation, physical touch, acts of service, receiving gifts, or quality time? Tailoring your expressions of affection to his particular needs can have a profound impact on his sense of being cherished and prioritized. For instance, if his love language is words of affirmation, a simple, heartfelt compliment about his character, his hard work, or his role as a father can be incredibly powerful. Leaving a sweet note in his lunch bag, sending a text message during the day just to say you're thinking of him, or verbally acknowledging his efforts and strengths can make a significant difference. If his love language is acts of service, taking on a chore that he typically handles without being asked, or preparing his favorite meal, can communicate your love in a tangible way.

The importance of this intentional prioritization extends beyond the marital dyad itself; it has a direct and profound impact on your children. When children witness their parents actively investing in their relationship, demonstrating love, respect, and consistent connection, they are learning invaluable lessons about healthy relationships. They see a model of commitment and mutual care that will shape their own future expectations and behaviors. A strong parental unit, where both mother and father are clearly valuing each other, provides a sense of security and stability that is foundational for a child's emotional development. Children raised in homes where the marital relationship is a priority are more likely to have secure attachments, better social skills, and a healthier understanding of love and commitment. Your efforts to nurture your marriage are, in essence, a significant part of nurturing your children.

Remember that intimacy in marriage is not static; it is a living, breathing entity that requires ongoing cultivation. It can ebb and flow, and the periods of intense family demands are precisely when this cultivation is most critical. It's easy to fall into the trap of thinking that once the children are older or once life settles down, you'll have more time to reconnect. However, this approach can be dangerous, as the habits of disconnection can become deeply ingrained. It's far more effective to make the investment now, even in small, manageable ways. Think of it as tending to a garden. Neglect it, and weeds will take over, choking out the delicate plants. Tend to it regularly, even with small gestures, and it will continue to bloom.

Consider also the power of shared experiences, even simple ones. Going for a walk together after dinner, even if it's just around the block, can provide a casual opportunity to talk and be together without the pressure of a formal "date." Or perhaps it's sharing a cup of coffee in the morning before the household wakes, or a quiet moment reading side-by-side in the evening. These shared moments create a sense of partnership and togetherness that is essential for a thriving marriage. It's about weaving your husband into the fabric of your daily life in meaningful ways, demonstrating that he is not just another person in the house, but the one with whom you share your life's deepest journey.

The biblical principle of "loving your neighbor as yourself" (Mark 12:31) finds its most intimate application within marriage. If we are to love our spouse well, we must first ensure that our own needs are not entirely neglected, allowing us to give from a place of abundance rather than depletion. However, even when feeling depleted, the intentional act of reaching out to your husband, of making an effort to connect, is a powerful act of love that often replenishes the giver as much as the receiver. It's a reciprocal dance, and sometimes, one partner has to take the lead in initiating that connection.

Furthermore, communicating your needs and desires for connection is also vital. While your husband should be discerning and attentive, you also have a responsibility to voice what you need. A simple, "Honey, I miss spending quality time with you. Could we plan a date night soon?" or "I'd love it if we could have just 15 minutes each day to talk without distractions," can open the door for him to respond and for you to work together to make it happen. Collaboration is key;

marriage is a team effort, and prioritizing each other's relational needs requires both partners to be actively involved.

In essence, prioritizing your husband is a continuous, active pursuit. It's about recognizing that the marital bond is a precious gift from God that requires diligent care. It's about making a conscious choice, day after day, to invest in your relationship, to nurture intimacy, and to foster a deep, abiding connection. Even when life feels overwhelming, and the demands seem insurmountable, remembering the foundational importance of your marriage will empower you to find those pockets of time, those moments of connection, that will keep your love strong and vibrant, a beautiful testament to God's design for marriage. It is in these intentional efforts that the true flourishing of your marriage, and indeed your entire family, will be found.

Effective communication is the lifeblood of any thriving marriage, and for us as Christian wives and mothers, it's also a sacred stewardship, a divine calling to build up our husbands and our homes. The previous discussion emphasized the vital importance of prioritizing our husbands amidst the beautiful, yet often demanding, rhythm of family life. We explored how intentional time, small daily check-ins, and personalized expressions of love can foster a deep and lasting connection. Now, we turn our attention to the *how* of maintaining and deepening that connection through the practice of speaking truth in love, a cornerstone of godly communication that transforms ordinary conversations into opportunities for profound intimacy and growth.

The world often presents communication as a battleground, a place where one either wins or loses, asserts dominance, or remains silent. However, our faith calls us to a different paradigm. Ephesians 4:29-31 paints a clear picture: "Let no corrupting talk come out of your mouths, but only such as is good for building up, as fits the occasion, that it may give grace to those who hear. And do not grieve the Holy Spirit of God, by whom you were sealed for the day of redemption.

Let all bitterness and wrath and anger and clamor and slander be put away from you, along with all malice." This is not merely advice; it's a directive for how we are to engage with one another, especially with the person God has joined us to. Building up, giving grace, and putting away negativity are the very essence of speaking truth in love within our marriages. It means our words should be constructive, aiming to edify and strengthen our husbands, rather than to tear down or criticize. This requires a conscious effort to filter our thoughts and emotions through the lens of Christ's love and wisdom.

One of the foundational pillars of effective communication is active listening. This goes far beyond simply hearing the words our husbands speak; it involves a deep commitment to understanding their perspective, their feelings, and their needs. In the whirlwind of domestic responsibilities, it's easy to multitask during conversations, mentally ticking off to-do lists or planning the next meal while our husbands are speaking. However, this fragmented attention can leave our husbands feeling unheard and unimportant, undermining the very connection we seek to build. Active listening demands our undivided attention. When your husband is talking, put down the dish towel, step away from the laundry basket, and turn your body to face him. Make eye contact, nod to show you are engaged, and resist the urge to interrupt or formulate your response while he is still speaking.

Beyond the physical cues, active listening involves asking clarifying questions and reflecting back what you've heard. Statements like, "So, if I understand correctly, you're feeling frustrated because the project at work is falling behind schedule?" or "It sounds like you're feeling overwhelmed by the financial responsibilities right now. Is that right?" demonstrate that you are not just passively receiving information but actively processing it and seeking to grasp its full meaning. This not only validates his feelings but also ensures that you are on the same page, preventing misunderstandings that can fester and create distance. Remember, the goal is not to "fix" the problem immediately, but to first understand and acknowledge his experience. Often, a listening ear and a compassionate heart are the most powerful tools we possess in helping our husbands feel supported and loved.

In conjunction with active listening, learning to express our own needs and desires clearly and respectfully is equally crucial. Many women, especially those accustomed to nurturing roles, struggle with articulating their own needs. We might fear appearing selfish or burdensome, or perhaps we've learned over time that our needs are often overlooked. However, the biblical model of marriage is one of partnership, a mutual exchange of love and support. Just as we are called to listen to our husbands, they are called to listen to us. When we fail to communicate our needs, we create an imbalance and deny our husbands the opportunity to meet them.

The key is to frame our needs in a way that is both honest and gracious. Instead of accusatory statements like, "You never help me with the kids' bedtime," try a gentler, more vulnerable approach: "Honey, I'm feeling really exhausted tonight, and I would so appreciate it if we could tackle the kids' bedtime routine together. It would really lighten my load." This statement focuses on your feelings and expresses a desire for collaboration, rather than placing blame. Similarly, if you feel a need for emotional connection, you might say, "I had a tough day today, and I'd love to just sit and talk with you for a few minutes when you have a moment. I really value your perspective." This approach invites him into your experience and opens the door for him to offer the support you need. It's about sharing your heart, not demanding compliance.

Conflict is an inevitable part of any relationship, and marriage is no exception. The way we navigate these disagreements, however, can either strengthen or weaken our marital bond. Our goal in conflict resolution is not to avoid disagreement altogether, but to handle it in a manner that honors God and fosters deeper understanding and intimacy. This is where the principle of speaking truth in love truly shines. 1 Corinthians 13:4-7 reminds us that "love is patient and kind... it is not irritable or resentful... it bears all things, believes all things, hopes all things, endures all things." When conflicts arise, we must ask ourselves if our words and actions are reflecting these qualities of love.

A vital aspect of constructive conflict resolution is to remain calm and focused on the issue at hand, rather than resorting to personal attacks or bringing up past grievances. This can be incredibly challenging when emotions are running high. When you feel yourself becoming overwhelmed or tempted to say something you'll regret, it is perfectly acceptable to call for a pause. "I'm feeling too upset to talk about this constructively right now. Can we take a 20-minute break and come back to this conversation?" This allows both of you to regain composure and approach the discussion with a clearer mind. During this break, instead of rehashing the argument, take time to pray, to self-reflect on your own contributions to the conflict, and to seek God's wisdom for how to proceed.

When you resume the conversation, aim for empathy. Try to understand the situation from your husband's point of view, even if you don't agree with it. Use "I" statements to express your feelings and needs, as previously discussed. For example, instead of saying, "You always leave your socks on the floor," which is accusatory and likely untrue, try, "I feel frustrated when socks are left on the floor because it makes the house feel cluttered, and I value a tidy space." This focuses on your feeling and your value, making it less confrontational and more open to a collaborative solution.

Furthermore, seeking to understand the underlying needs behind your husband's actions or words is crucial. Often, behavior that we perceive as negative is a misguided attempt to meet a legitimate need. Perhaps the socks on the floor are a sign of his exhaustion after a long day, or a reflection of a different upbringing regarding household order. By seeking to understand these underlying needs, we can address the root of the issue with compassion, rather than simply reacting to the surface behavior. This deepens our understanding of each other and strengthens our ability to work through challenges together.

Creating a safe space for open dialogue is paramount. This means fostering an environment where both husband and wife feel secure enough to be vulnerable, to express their true thoughts and feelings without fear of judgment, ridicule, or severe repercussions. As wives, we play a significant role in cultivating this safety. This involves our consistent responses, our willingness to listen without immediately jumping to conclusions, and our commitment to resolving conflict with grace and humility. When our husbands know that they can share their struggles, their doubts, and their mistakes with us without being met with condemnation, they are far more likely to be open and honest.

This safety extends to being a safe harbor for our husbands' emotions. In a world that often encourages men to suppress their feelings, our marriages should be a place where they can safely express a full range of emotions. If your husband expresses sadness, anger, or vulnerability, respond with empathy and understanding, not with dismissal or impatience. Ask questions like, "Tell me more about what's making you feel that way," or "How can I support you through this?" Your compassionate response can be a powerful balm, helping him feel truly seen and loved, and strengthening the emotional intimacy in your marriage.

The biblical principle of gentleness, as highlighted in Galatians 5:22-23, is a key component of speaking truth in love. Gentleness is not weakness; it is strength under control, a tender regard for the feelings of others, and a willingness to yield rather than to dominate.

When we speak to our husbands with gentleness, we communicate respect and value for them as individuals and as our partners. This might look like softening our tone of voice when discussing a sensitive topic, choosing our words carefully to avoid unnecessary harshness, or offering a comforting touch during a difficult conversation.

Consider the impact of our words on our husbands' spirit. Unkind, critical, or dismissive words can chip away at his self-esteem and his desire to connect with us. Conversely, words of affirmation, encouragement, and sincere appreciation can build him up and draw him closer. Philippians 4:8 encourages us to think about whatever is true, noble, right, pure, lovely, admirable, excellent, or praiseworthy. While this verse speaks to our thoughts, it also informs our speech. When we intentionally focus on the good qualities of our husbands and articulate those qualities, we are speaking life and encouragement into our marriage.

Another crucial element of effective communication is the ability to forgive and to seek forgiveness. No marriage is without its missteps and hurts. We will inevitably say or do things that wound our husbands, and he will do the same. The ability to offer and receive forgiveness is essential for healing and moving forward. Jesus commands us to forgive "seventy times seven" (Matthew 18:22), a directive that underscores the boundless nature of forgiveness. When your husband apologizes, accept it with genuine grace, and communicate that you are choosing to let go of the offense. Likewise, when you have wronged him, be swift to apologize sincerely and to seek his forgiveness. This practice of mutual forgiveness creates a culture of grace within the marriage, allowing for repair and renewed connection.

Furthermore, we must be mindful of the non-verbal cues we send. Our body language, facial expressions, and even our presence (or lack thereof) communicate volumes. A sigh of exasperation, an eye roll, or turning away while he's speaking can undermine even the most carefully chosen words. Conversely, a warm smile, a gentle touch on the arm, or a receptive posture can reinforce our verbal expressions of love and understanding. Being aware of our own non-verbal communication and being attentive to our husband's non-verbal signals can significantly enhance the quality of our interactions.

It's also important to acknowledge that communication styles can differ between men and women, and even between individuals. While generalizations can be unhelpful, understanding that your husband might process information differently, or express himself in ways that are not identical to yours, can foster patience and reduce misinterpretations. For example, some men may need time to process their thoughts before speaking, while others may be more inclined to verbalize their feelings as they arise. Recognizing and respecting these differences, rather than trying to force your husband to communicate in precisely the same way you do, can lead to more harmonious interactions.

Building bridges of understanding through communication is an ongoing process, not a destination. It requires consistent effort, a willingness to learn and grow, and a deep reliance on God's strength and wisdom. As we practice active listening, express our needs with grace, navigate conflicts constructively, and cultivate a safe space for dialogue, we are not just improving our communication skills; we are actively nurturing the intimacy and strength of our marital bond. These practices, rooted in the biblical principles of love, respect, and truth, are essential for building a marriage that truly flourishes, reflecting the love of Christ to our husbands, our families, and the world. It is through these intentional acts of speaking truth in love that we honor our covenant, strengthen our partnership, and create a legacy of godly communication that will impact generations to come. Remember, the goal is not perfection, but progress, and a heart fully surrendered to God's design for marriage, with every conversation an opportunity to draw closer to one another and to Him.

In the tapestry of marriage, while the threads of physical intimacy are undeniably vital, the true strength and beauty of the fabric are woven from a richer, more intricate blend of emotional, intellectual, and spiritual connections. As Christian wives, we are called to nurture not just the outward expressions of love, but the deep, unseen currents that bind our hearts to our husbands. This goes beyond shared routines and spoken affirmations; it delves into the very core of our beings, fostering a profound sense of togetherness that can withstand the inevitable storms of life and celebrate its abundant joys. Building this holistic intimacy is not a passive occurrence; it is an active, intentional pursuit, a stewardship of the sacred union God has created.

Emotional intimacy is the bedrock upon which all other forms of closeness are built. It is the willingness to be vulnerable, to share our inner world – our fears, our hopes, our insecurities, and our deepest joys – with our husbands, and to receive theirs with empathy and grace. This level of openness requires a safe space, a sanctuary where both partners feel seen, heard, and accepted, flaws and all. For many women, especially those accustomed to being the nurturers, expressing personal needs and emotional vulnerabilities can be a challenge. We might have been conditioned to believe that strength lies in self-sufficiency, or that our own emotional needs are secondary to those of our children or our husbands. However, a truly intimate marriage is a partnership of mutual emotional support. It's about creating an environment where your husband feels comfortable sharing his own struggles, his anxieties about work, his frustrations, or even his moments of doubt, without fear of judgment or criticism. This isn't about burdening him but about inviting him into the sacred space of your shared life. When your husband senses that his emotional landscape is a safe territory to explore with you, it deepens his trust and fosters an unparalleled sense of connection.

Consider the simple act of initiating a conversation about his day that goes beyond the superficial. Instead of just asking, "How was your day?" which often elicits a one-word answer, try to ask more specific, emotionally attuned questions. "What was the most challenging part of your day?" or "What brought you a sense of accomplishment today?" These prompts invite him to share not just events, but feelings. Similarly, when he shares a difficult experience, resist the urge to immediately offer solutions or platitudes. Sometimes, the greatest gift you can give is simply to listen, to offer a comforting touch, a validating nod, and empathetic words like, "That sounds incredibly frustrating," or "I can see why that would make you feel that way." This active, compassionate listening validates his feelings and communicates that his emotional well-being is a priority for you. It's in these moments of shared vulnerability that the emotional intimacy in a marriage truly blossoms, creating a bond that is resilient and deeply satisfying. Furthermore, expressing your own emotions openly, rather than expecting your husband to be a mind-reader, is crucial. When you've had a stressful day, instead of withdrawing or becoming irritable, try saying, "Honey, I'm feeling a bit overwhelmed today. Could we spend a few minutes just talking about it, or maybe just sit together quietly for a bit?" This vulnerability allows him to understand your needs and offers him the opportunity to minister to your heart, strengthening your mutual reliance and affection.

Intellectual intimacy, though perhaps less discussed, is equally essential for a flourishing marriage. This dimension involves engaging with each other's minds, sharing ideas, discussing beliefs, and exploring intellectual pursuits together. It's about respecting and valuing each other's thoughts and perspectives, even when they differ. In the busyness of life, it's easy for conversations to become superficial, revolving around logistics, chores, and the children's schedules. However, intentionally carving out time to engage in deeper intellectual dialogue can significantly enhance marital intimacy. This can manifest in various ways. It might involve reading the same book and then discussing its themes, characters, and impact on your own thinking. Or perhaps engaging in discussions about current events, political issues, or theological questions that pique your interest. For couples, this can involve sharing your thoughts on a sermon, a documentary, or even a historical event. It's about being curious about what's going on in your husband's mind, his intellectual journey, and what he finds meaningful and thought-provoking.

Consider the value of discussing your faith together. Engaging in Bible study as a couple, sharing insights from your personal devotions, or discussing how your faith impacts your daily decisions can create a powerful intellectual and spiritual bond. It's not about debating theological points to win, but about exploring the depths of God's Word together, seeking to understand its truths and how they apply to your lives and your marriage. This shared intellectual pursuit can be incredibly unifying, creating a common ground of understanding and purpose. Even simple acts, like discussing a news article that caught your eye or a concept you learned, can spark meaningful conversations that reveal your husband's intellect and provide opportunities for mutual learning. It's also about respecting each other's intellectual contributions. When your husband shares an idea or a perspective, listen attentively, ask clarifying questions, and offer your own thoughts thoughtfully. Avoid dismissing his ideas outright or dominating the conversation. This mutual respect for each other's intellect fosters an environment of shared growth and deeper connection, making your conversations not just exchanges of information, but opportunities to build a shared understanding of the world and your place within it. This intellectual engagement can also involve shared hobbies or interests that require problem-solving or creative thinking, further solidifying your partnership.

Spiritual intimacy is, for Christian couples, the apex of marital connection. It is the shared journey of faith, the mutual commitment to growing closer to God and to each other through Him. This dimension is about praying together, worshipping together, and actively supporting each other's spiritual growth. When a couple aligns their hearts and minds in pursuit of God, their marriage becomes a powerful testament to His love and faithfulness. The Bible encourages us to bear one another's burdens and to strengthen each other in our faith. This can be expressed in numerous practical ways.

One of the most impactful practices is praying together regularly. This doesn't have to be a lengthy, formal affair. It can be a few minutes before bed, a quick prayer before a meal, or even a dedicated time each week to share prayer requests and intercede for one another and for your family. When you pray together, you are not only bringing your concerns before God, but you are also reinforcing your unity as a couple before Him. It's a powerful act of surrender and trust. Sharing your prayer requests allows your husband to know how to best support you, and vice versa. It opens up avenues for comfort, encouragement, and spiritual guidance.

Beyond prayer, engaging in shared spiritual disciplines is crucial. This might include attending church services together, participating in a small group, or even reading devotional materials side-by-side. When you are both actively pursuing spiritual growth, you are naturally drawing closer to each other. Your conversations will be infused with discussions about your faith, your spiritual insights, and how you are striving to live out God's will. This shared spiritual pursuit creates a common purpose and a deeper understanding of each other's values and priorities.

Furthermore, spiritual intimacy involves holding each other accountable in a loving and supportive way. This doesn't mean being judgmental or critical but rather encouraging each other to stay on the path of faith. It might involve gently reminding your husband of a biblical principle or offering support when he is struggling with a particular sin. Similarly, he should be able to do the same for you. This mutual accountability, rooted in love and a desire for each other's spiritual well-being, is a hallmark of a Christ-centered marriage. It's about building each other up in the Spirit, helping one another to be more like Christ. Consider the power of sharing your spiritual insights or moments of God's presence with your husband. When you feel a particular passage of Scripture speak to your heart, share it with him. When you experience a moment of answered prayer or a profound sense of God's peace, share that joy with him. These shared spiritual experiences deepen your bond and create a shared spiritual heritage.

Nurturing intimacy in all these areas – emotional, intellectual, and spiritual – is not about achieving a perfect, static state of closeness. It is a dynamic, ongoing process that requires intentionality, effort, and a deep reliance on God. It means being willing to step outside of your comfort zone, to be vulnerable, and to invest time and energy into building a connection that transcends the physical. When these dimensions of intimacy are cultivated, the physical aspect of your marriage will also be enriched and deepened. It's a holistic approach to love, honoring the entirety of the person God has placed in your life as your partner. This commitment to building a multifaceted intimacy not only strengthens your marriage but also glorifies God, creating a beautiful reflection of His love for His church. It transforms your marriage from a mere companionship into a vibrant, thriving partnership, a true sanctuary where both husband and wife can grow, flourish, and experience the fullness of God's design for them.

Praying together is not merely an optional add-on to a healthy marriage; it is a fundamental spiritual discipline that actively cultivates unity, deepens faith, and invites the very presence of God into the heart of your union. It's a sacred act where two individuals, bound by covenant, intentionally align their hearts and voices before the Creator, acknowledging their mutual dependence on Him and on each other. This shared spiritual practice moves beyond individual devotion, creating a unique spiritual ecosystem within the marriage, a fertile ground where love, trust, and resilience can flourish. When couples commit to praying together, they are not just seeking divine intervention for their problems; they are actively building a shared spiritual heritage, a testimony of God's faithfulness woven into the very fabric of their marital journey. This practice serves as a powerful anchor, grounding the relationship in something far greater than their own strength or understanding, equipping them to navigate the complexities and challenges of life with a unified spirit and an unwavering hope. It transforms the marriage into a dynamic partnership, a testament to the power of God working within and through two lives joined together in love.

The journey of praying together as a couple is often a gradual one, especially for those new to the practice. It's essential to approach this sacred discipline with grace, patience, and a spirit of shared discovery rather than rigid expectation. Think of it as learning a new language together, where early conversations might be hesitant or even a little awkward, but with consistent effort and mutual encouragement, fluency and deep understanding will emerge. The most crucial first step is establishing a consistent rhythm, even if it's just for a few minutes each day. This consistency, more than duration, builds momentum and makes prayer a natural, integrated part of your marital life. Consider setting aside a specific time, perhaps before turning out the lights at night, after dinner, or first thing in the morning. Choose a time that is least likely to be interrupted and that works for both of you. The goal is not to add another stressful obligation to your already busy schedules, but to carve out a sacred space for connection – with God and with each other. This intentionality signals to your husband that his spiritual well-being, and your shared spiritual journey, is a priority. It's an investment in the deepest layer of your intimacy, one that yields eternal dividends.

When you first begin praying together, the content of your prayers might feel simple or even repetitive. This is perfectly normal. Start with expressions of gratitude for the day, for each other, and for the blessings God has bestowed. Thank Him for specific things – a child's laughter, a moment of peace, provision for your needs, or simply the gift of each other's presence. This practice of thanksgiving not only cultivates a more positive and optimistic outlook but also trains your hearts to recognize God's hand in the everyday details of your lives. As you grow more comfortable, begin to share your burdens and concerns. This is where the true strength of praying together begins to manifest. Instead of carrying anxieties alone, you bring them before God as a united front. Expressing your fears, your worries about finances, health, family, or work, allows your husband to not only hear your heart but also to stand with you in prayer. This sharing of vulnerabilities creates an unparalleled sense of emotional and spiritual solidarity. It's an unspoken declaration that you are a team, facing life's challenges not as isolated individuals, but as partners united in faith and purpose. When you articulate your struggles aloud to your husband in the presence of God, you are giving him the opportunity to intercede on your behalf, to offer comfort, and to strategize how you might face the challenge together. This communal prayer becomes a tangible expression of bearing one another's burdens, a core biblical injunction that strengthens the marital bond immeasurably.

Moreover, praying together provides a powerful avenue for celebrating blessings and victories. When God answers a prayer, whether it's for a job, healing, or a breakthrough in a difficult situation, take time to acknowledge it together in prayer. This shared act of praise and thanksgiving reinforces your faith in God's power and faithfulness. It creates a shared spiritual memory bank, a testament to the fact that God has been with you and has moved on your behalf. These moments of corporate thanksgiving solidify your trust in Him and encourage you to continue bringing all your concerns, big and small, before Him. It's a beautiful cycle: you share your needs, God answers, and you celebrate together, growing stronger in your faith and your unity as a couple. This shared spiritual journey, marked by both confession of weakness and celebration of divine strength, builds a profound and resilient connection that is impervious to the superficial storms of life.

To foster a deeper sense of partnership in prayer, consider adopting different roles or approaches. One of you might lead the prayer, while the other intercedes or adds specific points. Alternatively, you could take turns praying for specific areas of your life or family. For instance, one evening you might pray specifically for your children's spiritual growth, and the next evening for your husband's wisdom in his workplace. This variety keeps the practice fresh and ensures that both partners are actively engaged and contributing to your shared prayer life. It's also beneficial to discuss your prayer requests beforehand. This allows each person to prepare their heart and mind, and it ensures that you are praying in agreement and with a shared focus. When you share what is on your heart, your husband gains a deeper understanding of your inner world, and vice versa, fostering a more empathetic and connected prayer experience. This shared vulnerability and intentionality in prayer transforms it from a perfunctory duty into a deeply meaningful act of love and commitment.

The impact of praying together extends far beyond the immediate moment of prayer itself. It cultivates a spiritual synergy within the marriage, where the faith of one partner can uplift and strengthen the other. When one spouse is experiencing a season of spiritual dryness or doubt, the consistent prayer of the other can serve as a lifeline, holding them steady until their own faith can reignite. This mutual support in the spiritual realm is a profound expression of love, demonstrating a commitment to each other's eternal well-being. It's a visual representation of the biblical principle found in Ecclesiastes 4:9-12, which states, "Two are better than one, because they have a good return for their labor: If either of them falls down, one can help the other up. But pity anyone who falls and has no one to help them up. Though one may be overpowered, two can defend themselves. A cord of three strands is not quickly broken." In your marriage, that cord of three strands is you, your husband, and God, bound together by the discipline of prayer.

Furthermore, praying together allows you to invite God's presence into your marriage in a tangible way. As you align your hearts with His will through prayer, you create an atmosphere where His peace,

His wisdom, and His love can permeate your home and your relationship. This shared reliance on God fosters a deeper sense of security and belonging. You are not navigating life's uncertainties alone; you are doing so with the Almighty as your constant companion and guide. This shared spiritual journey cultivates an enduring sense of partnership, where decisions are made with prayerful consideration, and challenges are faced with a united reliance on God's strength. It builds a resilience that allows your marriage to withstand the inevitable trials of life, emerging stronger and more unified with each shared prayer experience.

It is also important to acknowledge that sometimes, praying together might feel challenging. There might be days when you feel disconnected, tired, or even frustrated with each other. On these occasions, prayer can feel like the last thing you want to do. However, it is precisely in these moments that shared prayer can be most transformative. It's a conscious choice to prioritize your marital covenant and your commitment to God, even when emotions are difficult. If you find yourselves struggling to connect in prayer, start with simple, honest prayers acknowledging your struggles. Pray for a softened heart, for patience, and for a renewed sense of connection with God and with each other. Even a brief, heartfelt prayer admitting your difficulty in praying together can be a powerful act of humility and dependence on God. Remember, God looks at the heart, and your willingness to engage in this discipline, even imperfectly, is a sacrifice that honors Him and strengthens your marriage. This consistent, intentional practice of praying together is a cornerstone of a Christ-centered marriage, a sacred discipline that fosters profound intimacy, unwavering unity, and an unshakeable reliance on the One who is the source of all love and strength.

Parents, by the very nature of our calling, are entrusted with a sacred and profound responsibility: to act as the primary spiritual guides for our children. This isn't a role we can delegate entirely to Sunday school teachers, youth pastors, or even the church community, though these are invaluable resources. The foundational shaping of a child's understanding of God, their relationship with Him, and their grasp of biblical truth begins within the home, under our loving and intentional guidance. The Bible itself provides a clear mandate for this. Deuteronomy 6:6-7 speaks directly to this, instructing parents, "These commandments that I give you today are to be upon your hearts. Impress them on your children. Talk about them when you sit at home and when you walk along the road, when you lie down and when you get up." This is not a suggestion; it's a directive woven into the very fabric of God's covenant with His people. It paints a vivid picture of faith being integrated into the entirety of daily life, not confined to a specific time or place. It calls for a pervasive, lived faith that permeates every aspect of our existence, and consequently, the existence of our children.

This biblical instruction underscores a fundamental truth: we are our children's first and most influential models of faith. Long before they can fully articulate theological concepts or grasp abstract spiritual principles, they are absorbing our attitudes, our reactions, and our devotion. They watch how we navigate challenges, how we express gratitude, how we extend forgiveness, and how we talk about God. If our faith is vibrant, present, and authentic, it will naturally spill over into their lives. Conversely, if our faith is merely a Sunday performance, or if it's something we rarely discuss or demonstrate in our daily routines, our children will likely perceive it as such. This means that our own spiritual walk is not a private matter when we are parents; it becomes a public testament, an ongoing sermon preached through our actions and our words. It requires us to be intentional about living out our faith in ways that are visible and understandable to our children. It means praying not just in private but also demonstrating prayer in our daily lives, talking about God's goodness not just on the mountaintop but also in the valley, and showing grace not just to those who are easy to love but also to those who might be difficult. Our spiritual life becomes a blueprint for theirs, and the foundation we lay is critical for the structure that will be built upon it.

To effectively guide our children spiritually, we must move beyond simply imparting information and instead focus on nurturing a relationship. This means helping them understand who God is, not just as a distant Creator, but as a loving Father who desires intimacy with them. This begins with us having that intimate relationship ourselves. When we speak of God's love, His mercy, and His faithfulness, it carries far more weight when our children see and experience these qualities reflected in our own lives and in our interactions with them. Consider the way a child learns to trust. They learn it through consistent care, through promises kept, and through knowing that their needs will be met. So too, they learn to trust God through our consistent prayers for them, through our reliance on His provision, and through our willingness to share our own faith journey – including the times we have wrestled with doubt or faced difficult circumstances but ultimately found God's strength. This process of spiritual guidance is not a one-time event, but an ongoing, dynamic journey that evolves as the child grows. It requires patience, a willingness to adapt our approach, and a deep dependence on the Holy Spirit to lead and empower us.

The integration of faith into everyday life is paramount. Deuteronomy 6's instruction to talk about God's commands "when you sit at home and when you walk along the road, when you lie down and when you get up" is a powerful reminder that spiritual discipleship is not confined to formal lessons or religious services. It's about weaving faith into the fabric of ordinary moments. This can manifest in countless ways. For instance, during mealtimes, we can pause to thank God for the food, acknowledging His provision and expressing gratitude. We can talk about the attributes of God as we observe His creation – the beauty of a sunset, the intricate design of a flower, or the vastness of the night sky. When a child experiences disappointment, rather than dismissing their feelings, we can gently guide them to understand that God is with them in their sadness and can bring comfort and strength. When they exhibit kindness or generosity, we can point to these actions as reflections of God's own character and encourage them to continue acting in such ways. It's about making faith a natural part of conversation, a consistent presence that shapes their understanding of the world and their place within it.

This intentionality also involves teaching children how to pray. It's not enough to tell them to pray; we need to show them how. Start with simple, repetitive prayers, like a "grace before meals" prayer, or a bedtime prayer of thanks. As they grow, encourage them to express their own thoughts and feelings to God. This might involve writing prayers, drawing pictures of what they are praying about, or simply talking aloud to God. We can model different types of prayer: prayers of confession, prayers of thanksgiving, prayers of petition, and prayers of intercession for others. It is also beneficial to involve children in praying for specific needs within the family or for others in their community. This teaches them that prayer is a powerful tool for communication with God and a way to actively participate in His work in the world. When children see that prayer is a regular, meaningful part of our lives, they are more likely to embrace it as their own.

Furthermore, parents have a critical role in helping children understand the Bible. This doesn't necessarily mean starting with complex theological treatises. Begin with age-appropriate stories that highlight God's character, His promises, and His love for humanity. Use visual aids, storybooks, and even simple memorization of key verses. As children mature, introduce them to the narrative arc of Scripture, helping them see how God's plan of redemption unfolds from Genesis to Revelation. Discuss how biblical principles apply to their everyday lives – how to handle conflict with siblings according to biblical wisdom, how to be honest and trustworthy, how to show compassion to those in need. Explaining *why* certain commands are given, and how they reflect God's desire for our good, can foster a deeper understanding and appreciation for His Word. It's about making the Bible come alive, not just as a historical document, but as a living, relevant guide for their lives.

Our home should be a sanctuary where faith is nurtured and where children feel safe to explore their questions and doubts about God. This requires us to be approachable and open to their inquiries, even if they are challenging. Instead of shutting down difficult questions, we should view them as opportunities to delve deeper into God's truth together. If we don't have all the answers, it's perfectly acceptable to say so and then commit to finding the answer together, perhaps by researching in the Bible or consulting with a trusted spiritual mentor. This honesty builds trust and demonstrates that faith is a journey of ongoing discovery, not a static set of doctrines. It also models humility, a crucial Christian virtue. When children see their parents actively seeking to understand God more fully, they are more likely to develop a similar hunger for truth.

The spiritual formation of our children is intimately linked to our own spiritual growth. As we strive to be better spiritual guides, we are often stretched and challenged in our own faith. We might need to deepen our understanding of Scripture, cultivate greater patience, or learn to rely more fully on God's grace. This journey of spiritual parenting is one of mutual discipleship. Our commitment to raising our children in the ways of the Lord propels us forward in our own walk with Him. It's a beautiful synergy, where our desire to lead them closer to God also draws us closer to Him. This means prioritizing our own spiritual disciplines – prayer, Bible study, fellowship – not out of obligation, but out of a genuine desire to be spiritually healthy for ourselves and for our family. A spiritually vibrant parent is far better equipped to nurture spiritual vibrancy in their children.

It is also important to recognize that every child is unique, with different temperaments, learning styles, and spiritual aptitudes. What resonates with one child may not resonate with another. Therefore, our approach to spiritual guidance needs to be flexible and adaptable. We need to observe our children, understand their individual needs, and tailor our methods accordingly. Some children may be drawn to music and worship, while others might connect more through service or intellectual exploration of faith. The key is to discover what ignites their spiritual curiosity and to fan that flame. This might involve exploring different expressions of worship, engaging them in age-appropriate service projects, or providing them with resources that cater to their specific interests. The goal is to help them develop a personal, authentic faith that is their own, not just a reflection of ours.

Ultimately, the role of parents as spiritual guides is about cultivating a deep, abiding love for God and a desire to follow Him. It's about planting seeds of faith, watering them with consistent spiritual nurture, and trusting God to bring about the growth. It's a marathon, not a sprint, filled with moments of great joy and occasional struggle. By modeling authentic faith, integrating spiritual truths into daily life, teaching them how to connect with God through prayer and His Word, and creating a home where faith is cherished, we are fulfilling our God-given mandate to raise children who love and honor the Lord. This is one of the most significant and rewarding aspects of our calling as parents, a legacy that extends far beyond this earthly life. It requires intentionality, consistency, and an unwavering reliance on God's grace to equip us for this vital task.

The beauty of integrating spiritual practices into the rhythm of family life is that it doesn't require elaborate planning or professional theological degrees. It's about intentionality and creating opportunities for God to be present and acknowledged in the everyday. For families with young children, the key is simplicity and engagement. Think about how we naturally involve our little ones in other aspects of life – cooking, playing, reading stories.

Spiritual formation can and should be approached with the same natural, joyful integration.

Consider the humble family mealtime. It's a built-in opportunity for spiritual connection. Before the first bite, a simple "grace" can transform a mundane meal into a moment of thanksgiving. This doesn't need to be a lengthy, formal prayer. For toddlers, it might be as short as, "Thank you, God, for the yummy food! Amen." As they grow, you can introduce more elements, perhaps thanking God for the farmers who grew the food, or for bringing the family together. This practice, repeated consistently, instills gratitude and acknowledges God's provision. Beyond a prayer of thanks, mealtimes can become natural settings for discussing biblical truths. Did someone share a kind act at school? You can connect that to the biblical principle of loving your neighbor. Is there a challenge one of the children faced? You can explore how biblical figures handled similar situations, or how God's strength can be found in difficult times. These conversations, woven into the fabric of daily life, make faith relevant and accessible.

Storytelling is another powerful tool. The Bible is rich with narratives that capture the imagination and teach profound truths. For young children, this means focusing on the core message and using age-appropriate language and resources. Picture Bibles, flannelgraph stories, or even simple dramatic reenactments can bring biblical accounts to life. Instead of just reading the story of Noah's Ark, encourage your children to draw the animals, build a miniature ark out of blocks, or even sing a song about the journey. When teaching about David and Goliath, discuss courage and faith, and perhaps have a friendly "target practice" with soft balls, linking it to David's skill with a sling. The goal is not to present a dry historical account, but to help children understand the character of God, His faithfulness, and His love through these stories. As they mature, you can delve deeper into the theological implications, but the foundation of engaging storytelling is crucial.

Prayer, as mentioned previously, is the direct line of communication with our Heavenly Father. For children, learning to pray can be a gradual process. Start with modeling. Let them see you pray, not just in moments of crisis, but in everyday instances. Pray for a lost item, pray for a friend who is sick, pray for wisdom before making a decision. When you pray with your children, start with simple requests. "God, thank you for this sunny day." "God, please help Mommy feel better." Encourage them to express their own prayers, even if they are short or seem simple. You can also introduce different types of prayer through creative means. For a prayer of confession, you might use a "confession jar" where they can write down or draw something they did wrong, and then together, you can pray for forgiveness. For prayers of thanksgiving, a "gratitude tree" where each family member writes something they are thankful for on a leaf and hangs it on a drawing of a tree can be a visual reminder of God's blessings. These activities make prayer an active, participatory experience, rather than a passive recitation.

Creating a family worship time, even if it's just for 15-20 minutes a few times a week, can be incredibly impactful. The beauty of this time is its flexibility. It doesn't have to be a rigid, formal service. It can be a blend of singing praise songs, reading a short Bible passage, discussing its meaning, and praying together. For very young children, keep the Bible reading brief and engaging. A single verse or a short story from a children's Bible will suffice. You might follow this with a lively worship song that encourages movement and participation. As they grow, you can introduce more in-depth discussion, asking them questions like, "What does this verse tell us about God?" or "How can we apply this to our lives today?" The key is to make it a positive, anticipated time. If it becomes a chore, children will disengage.

Establishing consistent spiritual routines and traditions acts as the scaffolding for faith development within the home. These aren't just activities; they are tangible expressions of a faith-filled life that children will internalize and, hopefully, carry into their own families. Think about holidays and special occasions. How can these be infused with a Christ-centered focus? Christmas is a natural time to emphasize the birth of Jesus through nativity scenes, special readings from Luke, and carols that focus on the Incarnation. Easter can be about celebrating the resurrection, perhaps with an egg hunt that symbolizes new life, followed by a discussion of Jesus' victory over death.

Beyond the major holidays, consider creating smaller, recurring traditions. A "faith walk" could be a weekly or monthly outing where you go to a park or nature trail and discuss God's creation, thanking Him for the beauty around you. A "prayer journal" that family members contribute to, jotting down prayer requests and answers, can become a cherished record of God's faithfulness. Even something as simple as a dedicated "prayer corner" in your home, with comfortable cushions, a Bible, and perhaps a candle, can signal that this is a special space for connecting with God.

The power of tradition lies in its predictability and its ability to create shared memories. When children know that every Sunday evening involves reading a chapter of a book like "The Pilgrim's Progress" (adapted for their age, of course) or that every Friday night is "Family Worship and Pizza Night," it builds anticipation and reinforces the importance of these spiritual anchors. These traditions become a comforting constant in their lives, a reminder that their family's foundation is built on something solid and eternal. They also provide opportunities for bonding, for laughter, and for open communication, all within the context of growing closer to God together.

It's important to remember that consistency is more important than perfection. There will be days when the energy isn't there, when schedules are chaotic, or when children are resistant. On those days, do what you can. A quick prayer before bed, a shared moment of singing a song, or a brief discussion about God's love is far better than abandoning the effort altogether. The goal is to cultivate a culture of faith, not to achieve a flawless execution of a spiritual program. Children are remarkably perceptive; they will understand that life is not always perfect, but they will also see your commitment and your love for God, and that is a powerful witness in itself.

Furthermore, involving children in the planning and execution of family devotions can increase their engagement and ownership. Ask them what songs they want to sing, what Bible stories they are interested in hearing, or what they want to pray for. This empowers them and helps them see that their contributions are valued. It also allows you to tailor the devotions to their current interests and developmental stages. What captivates a four-year-old might be different from what engages a ten-year-old. Flexibility and responsiveness are key.

The objective of these practices is not to create little theologians overnight, but to foster a deep-seated love for Jesus and a comfortable, ongoing relationship with Him. It's about helping them see that faith isn't just a set of rules or doctrines, but a vibrant, living relationship with a God who loves them intimately and desires to walk with them through every aspect of their lives. By intentionally weaving these spiritual practices into the fabric of your family's daily existence, you are building a legacy of faith that will endure far beyond childhood. These simple, consistent acts of devotion become the building blocks of a strong spiritual foundation, nurturing hearts that are anchored in God's unchanging love and truth, creating cherished memories that will echo through generations.

Building a strong spiritual foundation for our children begins with intentionally teaching them the core truths of the Bible. This isn't about overwhelming them with complex theological doctrines, but rather about introducing them to the fundamental principles of God's character and His plan for humanity in ways that resonate with their understanding and stage of development. Our aim is to help them grasp, in simple yet profound terms, who God is, what He has done, and how they can live in relationship with Him. This foundational teaching forms the bedrock upon which their faith will be built and nurtured throughout their lives.

One of the most crucial truths to impart is the immeasurable love of God. This is not a conditional love, earned through good behavior, but a love that is freely given, encompassing and unconditional. We can introduce this concept through various means. Reading from the Gospels, particularly passages that describe Jesus interacting with children – welcoming them, blessing them, and speaking of the Kingdom of Heaven in terms of their innocence – can be incredibly impactful. For very young children, a simple story about God's love, perhaps illustrating it with the warmth of the sun or the embrace of a parent, can be a starting point. As they grow, we can explain that God's love is demonstrated most clearly through the sacrifice of His Son, Jesus Christ. This leads to the next foundational truth: salvation through Jesus.

Teaching about Jesus as our Savior is central to Christian faith. We need to explain that because of sin, humanity is separated from God. However, God, in His great love, sent His only Son, Jesus, to bridge that gap. Jesus lived a perfect life, died on the cross to pay the penalty for our sins, and rose again, conquering death. This is the essence of the Gospel. For children, this narrative can be shared through age-appropriate Bible stories. The story of Jesus' birth, His miracles, His death, and His resurrection are all vital components. Visual aids can be particularly helpful here. A simple drawing depicting Jesus on the cross, with an explanation of why He was there, or a craft project illustrating the empty tomb, can help solidify this message. Emphasize that accepting Jesus as Lord and Savior is how we receive forgiveness and eternal life. This is not a complex theological debate but a joyous announcement of God's good news.

We can use analogies that children understand, like a superhero coming to rescue people, or a doctor healing a sickness. The key is to convey the magnitude of God's love and Jesus' sacrifice in a way that is both accurate and accessible.

Forgiveness is another cornerstone of our faith, and it's essential that children understand both God's forgiveness of them and their need to forgive others. When we teach children about Jesus' sacrifice, we can connect it directly to the forgiveness of sins. God forgives us because Jesus paid the price. This means that no matter what they have done wrong, they can come to God, confess their sin, and receive His forgiveness. We can reinforce this through prayer, encouraging them to confess their wrongdoings and ask for forgiveness. Furthermore, we must teach them the importance of forgiving others, just as Christ has forgiven us. When a sibling or friend hurts them, we can gently guide them to remember how God has forgiven them and encourage them to extend that same grace. This is a difficult concept, even for adults, so it requires patience and consistent modeling. Stories from the Bible where forgiveness is demonstrated, such as Joseph forgiving his brothers, can be powerful teaching tools.

Obedience is not presented as a burdensome obligation but as a natural outflow of love and trust in God. When children understand that God loves them and desires the best for them, obedience becomes an act of love and a way to honor Him. We can teach this by explaining that God's commands are not meant to restrict them, but to protect them and guide them into a fulfilling life. Just as parents set boundaries for their children's safety and well-being, God's word provides guidance for our spiritual health. We can connect obedience to the fruit of the Spirit, explaining that when we obey God, we experience joy, peace, and love. Stories of biblical figures who obeyed God, like Noah building the ark or Abraham leaving his homeland, can illustrate the blessings that come from obedience. It is also important to teach that even when we fail to obey, God's grace is available, and we can ask for His help to live in obedience.

To effectively teach these foundational biblical truths, we need to employ a variety of methods that engage children's senses and minds. Storytelling remains a paramount tool. The Bible is replete with narratives that captivate and teach. Children are naturally drawn to stories, and by presenting biblical accounts in an engaging and age-appropriate manner, we can imbue them with profound spiritual lessons. Using children's Bibles with vibrant illustrations, acting out simple Bible stories, or even using puppets can bring these ancient texts to life. For instance, when teaching about God's provision, the story of the feeding of the five thousand can be a powerful illustration. We can discuss how Jesus took what little the disciples had and multiplied it to feed a vast crowd, highlighting God's ability to do far more than we can ask or imagine. This can be reinforced by discussing how God provides for our family's needs.

Songs are another powerful medium for teaching biblical truths. Music has a unique ability to lodge itself in our hearts and minds, and children are particularly responsive to it. There are countless praise and worship songs available that are specifically designed for children, teaching them about God's love, Jesus' sacrifice, and the importance of faith in simple, memorable lyrics. Singing these songs together during family devotions or even during everyday activities can reinforce these truths throughout the week. A song about God's love can be sung while preparing a meal, or a song about Jesus' resurrection can be part of a bedtime routine. The repetition inherent in music helps solidify these foundational concepts in a child's mind.

Visual aids can significantly enhance a child's comprehension and retention of biblical truths. This could include everything from simple drawings and crafts to more elaborate presentations. For example, when teaching about the Trinity, a simple diagram showing three distinct persons in one Godhead, perhaps using overlapping circles or a simple triangle, can be introduced as they mature. When discussing the concept of prayer, creating a dedicated prayer corner with a Bible, some comfortable cushions, and perhaps a picture of Jesus, can visually reinforce the importance of prayer. Crafting a "grace chart" where children can draw or write what they are thankful for before meals can be a visual reminder of God's provision and the importance of gratitude. These visual elements serve as tangible anchors for abstract spiritual concepts.

When introducing the concept of sin, it's important to define it simply as disobedience to God or doing wrong things. A visual representation of a broken relationship, perhaps a picture of two people separated by a gap, can illustrate how sin separates us from God. Then, introducing Jesus as the bridge that closes that gap can visually represent salvation. For the concept of the Holy Spirit, one might use a visual of a light bulb turning on in a dark room to signify enlightenment and guidance, or a gentle breeze to represent His presence. These visuals, when coupled with simple explanations and consistent repetition, help build a robust understanding of core biblical tenets.

The ultimate goal in teaching these foundational truths is to cultivate a deep and abiding love for God and a personal relationship with Jesus Christ. It is about nurturing hearts that are anchored in truth and are equipped to navigate the complexities of life with faith. By intentionally weaving these essential biblical concepts into the fabric of our family's daily life, we are not merely imparting information but shaping hearts and minds for eternity. These simple, consistent acts of teaching become the building blocks of a strong spiritual foundation, nurturing children who know, love, and serve the Lord.

As children grow, these foundational truths need to be revisited and deepened. What begins as a simple understanding of God's love might evolve into a more profound appreciation for His grace and mercy. The concept of salvation through Jesus, initially presented as a rescue from sin, can later be understood in terms of the transforming power of Christ's resurrected life. Forgiveness, once learned as a personal act, can expand to encompass compassion and empathy for all people. Obedience, initially framed as following rules, can mature into a desire to honor God in all aspects of life. This continuous engagement ensures that faith remains a living, breathing reality, not a static set of beliefs.

We must remember that our children are observing not only what we say but how we live. Our own consistent walk with God, our response to challenges, our interactions with others – all of these serve as powerful teaching moments. When they see us praying with sincerity, forgiving readily, and demonstrating obedience to God, even when it's difficult, they witness the practical outworking of these biblical truths. This authentic embodiment of faith is often more impactful than any spoken lesson. It's a living testimony that resonates deeply and leaves an indelible mark on their spiritual journey.

Furthermore, we must foster an environment where questions are encouraged, and doubts can be addressed with grace and patience. Children will inevitably encounter moments of confusion or uncertainty as they grapple with spiritual concepts. Creating a safe space for them to voice these questions, without fear of judgment or dismissal, is crucial. Our responses should be characterized by humility, acknowledging that we too are on a journey of faith and may not have all the answers. However, we can commit to seeking answers together, demonstrating a reliance on God and His Word as our ultimate source of truth. This collaborative approach to learning strengthens their trust in God and in our guidance.

The consistent reinforcement of these core biblical principles through various means – storytelling, music, visual aids, and most importantly, our own example – lays the essential groundwork for a life of faith. It equips our children with the spiritual vocabulary and understanding they need to build a personal relationship with God and to navigate the world with a biblical worldview. This intentional teaching is a profound investment in their eternal well-being, shaping them into individuals who not only know the truth but live it out with love and conviction.

The journey of raising children in the ways of the Lord is multifaceted, encompassing not only the foundational teachings of Scripture but also the practical application of godly principles in our daily interactions. Among the most crucial of these is the art of discipline, a topic often misunderstood and sometimes approached with trepidation. Yet, as we delve into the wisdom of God's Word, we discover that discipline, when rightly understood and applied, is not a punitive measure but a profound expression of love, a vital tool for shaping character, and an essential component in nurturing our children's spiritual growth. It is a practice that, when rooted in love and grace, fosters security, teaches valuable life lessons, and ultimately draws our children closer to the heart of God.

Our understanding of discipline must first be firmly anchored in the character of God Himself. He is our perfect Father, and His discipline of us, His children, is always motivated by love and aimed at our ultimate good. The author of Hebrews reminds us, "My son, do not make light of the Lord's discipline, and do not lose heart when he rebukes you, because the Lord disciplines the one, he loves, and he chastens everyone he accepts as his son." (Hebrews 12:5-6, NIV). This divine example sets the standard for our own parental discipline. It is not born out of frustration, anger, or a desire to exert control for its own sake. Instead, it flows from a deep wellspring of love, a commitment to guiding our children toward righteousness, and a desire to see them flourish into the individuals God created them to be. This understanding shifts our perspective from seeing discipline as a chore or a punishment to recognizing it as a sacred trust, a privilege to participate in God's loving work in our children's lives.

When discipline is rooted in love, it transforms the very atmosphere of our homes. Children who experience consistent, loving discipline feel secure. They learn to trust that while their actions may have consequences, the underlying relationship with their parents is unwavering and loving. This security is the fertile ground upon which healthy emotional and spiritual development can flourish. It allows them to explore, to make mistakes, and to learn from them without the crippling fear of rejection. This is a far cry from the emotional damage that can be inflicted by harsh, erratic, or fear-based discipline, which often breeds rebellion, resentment, or a deep-seated insecurity that can linger into adulthood. Our goal is not to break their spirit but to guide it, to mold it, and to help them understand the boundaries that protect and nurture them.

The grace aspect of discipline is equally crucial. Just as God extends grace to us through Jesus Christ, we are called to extend grace to our children. This means that when they err, we respond not with condemnation but with understanding, patience, and an opportunity for restoration. Grace-filled discipline acknowledges that our children are imperfect, just as we are. It recognizes that they will make mistakes, stumble, and sometimes choose the wrong path. In these moments, our response should be one of gentle correction, leading them back to the right way with kindness. This doesn't mean condoning their behavior but rather addressing it in a way that preserves their dignity and reinforces God's own abundant grace. We can explain, for example, that just as God forgives us when we confess our wrongdoing, they too can be forgiven, and they are called to forgive others. This teaching of grace in action builds within them a capacity for empathy, compassion, and a reliance on God's merciful heart.

Setting clear boundaries is a foundational element of loving discipline. Children thrive when they know what is expected of them and what the consequences are for crossing those lines. These boundaries are not arbitrary rules designed to stifle their freedom but are rather like guardrails on a highway, guiding them safely and preventing them from veering off into danger. When we establish these boundaries, we do so with clear communication. Explaining the

why behind a rule, even to young children, helps them understand the logic and purpose, making them more likely to respect it. For instance, a boundary around screen time might be explained by saying, "We limit screen time so you have plenty of energy to play outside, build with your blocks, and read good books, which helps your brain grow strong." This connects the boundary to a positive outcome, rather than simply stating a prohibition.

Consistency is the cornerstone of effective boundary-setting. When boundaries are enforced inconsistently, children become confused and may learn to push the limits, testing to see if a rule will be upheld today or disregarded. This inconsistency can create anxiety for a child, as they are never quite sure of the expectations. Our commitment to consistent discipline, however, should not be mistaken for rigidity. There are times when understanding the circumstances and applying wisdom is necessary. But the general rule should be that boundaries are clear, communicated, and consistently upheld. This doesn't mean we never adjust our approach as a child matures or as specific situations arise, but rather that the underlying principles and expectations remain stable.

Teaching responsibility is an integral part of discipline. As children grow, we can gradually introduce age-appropriate chores and tasks that contribute to the functioning of the household. This could start with simple tasks for toddlers, such as putting toys away in a designated bin, and progress to more complex responsibilities for older children, like helping with meal preparation or yard work. The purpose of assigning these tasks goes beyond simply getting the work done; it is about instilling in them a sense of contribution, ownership, and the understanding that everyone in the family has a role to play. When children understand that their efforts are valued and that they are contributing members of the family unit, it fosters a sense of purpose and self-worth. We can frame these responsibilities not as punishments, but as opportunities to serve and to learn valuable life skills. For example, explaining that helping to set the table is a way of showing love and care for the family can make the task more meaningful.

When it comes to correcting behavior, our approach should be measured and instructive. The Bible encourages us to correct with gentleness and patience. Proverbs 15:1 states, "A gentle answer turns away wrath, but a harsh word stirs up anger." This principle is vital in our interactions with our children. When a child misbehaves, our immediate reaction might be frustration, but we must take a moment to pause, pray for wisdom and patience, and then respond with a calm, firm, and loving correction. This might involve a conversation explaining why their behavior was wrong, helping them understand the impact of their actions on others, and guiding them toward a better choice. For younger children, this correction might be a simple redirecting of their attention or a brief timeout to calm down and reflect. For older children, it might involve a more in-depth discussion about their choices and the underlying reasons for their behavior.

Natural and logical consequences are powerful tools in teaching children about accountability. Natural consequences are those that occur as a direct result of a child's actions without parental intervention. For example, if a child leaves their favorite toy outside, the natural consequence might be that it gets wet from the rain or dirty from the mud. Logical consequences are those that parents set up to directly relate to the misbehavior. If a child refuses to tidy their room, a logical consequence might be that they lose the privilege of playing with their toys until the room is clean. The key to using consequences effectively is that they are clearly communicated beforehand, are reasonable in relation to the offense, and are consistently applied. This helps children connect their actions with their outcomes, fostering a sense of responsibility and teaching them to think through the potential results of their choices.

The ultimate aim of all our disciplinary efforts is to cultivate self-control and a God-honoring character. Discipline is not about creating perfect robots, but about nurturing individuals who can make wise choices, manage their emotions, and live lives that are pleasing to God. This process takes time, patience, and a deep reliance on the Holy Spirit to guide our words and actions. As we consistently apply love, grace, clear boundaries, and consistent correction, we are building a framework within our children that helps them learn to govern themselves. They begin to internalize these principles, not just as external rules to be followed, but as internal guides for their behavior and decision-making. This internal compass is what true discipline seeks to foster.

Furthermore, the parent-child relationship is strengthened, not weakened, by this kind of discipline. When children see that their parents are willing to take the time to correct them, to explain things, and to guide them through their mistakes, it communicates that they are deeply valued and loved. This process of correction, when done with gentleness and grace, builds trust. They learn that their parents are a safe harbor, a place where they can be honest about their struggles and receive support. This is in stark contrast to a home where discipline is absent or abusive, which can create fear and a breakdown of communication. Our discipline, therefore, should be an opportunity to draw closer to our children, to understand them better, and to deepen the bond of love and trust that is so essential to a healthy family.

In practice, this might look like responding to a toddler's tantrum not with mirroring anger, but with a calm presence, a gentle hand, and words that acknowledge their feelings while still upholding the boundary. "I see you are very upset because you can't have another cookie. It's hard when we have to wait. But we have already had our cookie for today, and it's time for dinner." This response validates their emotions while gently reinforcing the rule. For an older child who has lied, the discipline might involve a conversation about the importance of honesty, the disappointment their lie has caused, and a consequence that reinforces the value of truth, perhaps losing a privilege that requires trust. The focus remains on teaching and restoring, not on punishment for punishment's sake.

We must also be mindful of our own hearts and motivations when disciplining. Are we reacting out of impatience, frustration, or a desire to vent our own stress? Or are we responding with the heart of Christ, seeking to guide and nurture? This self-examination is crucial. If we find ourselves consistently reacting in anger, it's a signal to pause, seek God's help, and perhaps re-evaluate our approach. Our children are keenly aware of our emotional state, and they will learn from our responses. Modeling emotional regulation and self-control in our own lives is a powerful aspect of teaching discipline. When they see us making mistakes and then seeking forgiveness or making amends, they learn valuable lessons about humility and accountability.

The spiritual dimension of discipline is paramount. As Christians, we understand that our ultimate goal is to raise children who love and serve the Lord. Discipline, therefore, becomes a means to this end. It is about teaching them to align their wills with God's will, to understand the importance of obedience not as a burden but as an act of worship, and to recognize their need for God's grace and strength. When we correct a child, we can, at appropriate moments, connect the behavior to biblical principles. For example, if a child is acting selfishly, we can gently remind them of Jesus' example of selfless service and encourage them to consider how they can be more like Him. This integrates spiritual truth into the practical matter of correcting behavior, making discipline a discipleship opportunity.

Teaching children to take responsibility for their actions also involves helping them learn to apologize sincerely and to make amends when they have wronged someone. This is a crucial step in the restoration process after a disciplinary incident. A genuine apology involves acknowledging the wrong, expressing remorse, and a commitment to not repeat the behavior. Helping a child craft such an apology and then encouraging them to follow through on their words, teaches them the importance of reconciliation and the restorative power of repentance. This also provides an opportunity to reinforce the biblical concept of forgiveness, both in receiving it from others and extending it.

The process of discipline is ongoing, evolving as our children grow and mature. What is appropriate discipline for a two-year-old will look very different from what is appropriate for a teenager. Our approach must remain flexible, responsive to their developmental stages, and always guided by wisdom from God's Word and prayer. It is a marathon, not a sprint, and there will be moments of progress and moments of regression. Through it all, our unwavering commitment to discipline rooted in love and grace will lay a strong foundation for their character, their relationship with us, and most importantly, their relationship with our Heavenly Father. It is in this consistent, loving guidance that we fulfill our calling to raise children in the ways of the Lord.

Our children are our most precious earthly treasures, and the responsibility of nurturing them in the ways of the Lord is a sacred trust. While the Word of God provides the bedrock of our teachings, the living, breathing testament of our own lives serves as the most potent sermon. What we *do*, perhaps more than what we *say*, shapes the spiritual landscape of their hearts and minds. This is the essence of modeling a life of faith and integrity – it is the authentic embodiment of the truths we endeavor to impart, a continuous, conscious demonstration of a life surrendered to Christ.

Children are astute observers, absorbing the nuances of our character and the genuineness of our convictions with an almost uncanny precision. They learn from the quiet moments as much as from the grand pronouncements. When we speak of the importance of prayer, but our lives are devoid of regular, heartfelt communion with God, our words can ring hollow. Conversely, when they witness us consistently seeking God's presence in both the mundane and the momentous, they see prayer not as a ritual, but as a vital lifeline. They observe us wrestling with difficult decisions, not in isolation, but by first bringing them before the Lord, seeking His wisdom and guidance. This tangible act of reliance communicates a profound truth: that God is not a distant deity, but an ever-present Father who hears and answers. Imagine a moment where a significant family challenge arises – a job loss, a health concern, or even a relational conflict. If, in the face of this, our immediate reaction is panic or despair, our children will absorb that message. But if, instead, they see us turn to Scripture, fall to our knees in prayer, and approach the situation with a spirit of trust and reliance on God, they are witnessing faith in action. They learn that even amidst adversity, there is a source of strength and peace that transcends circumstances. This modeling is not about presenting a façade of perfection; rather, it is about demonstrating reliance on God's grace when we inevitably fall short.

Integrity is another cornerstone of a life of faith that children learn through observation. This means our words align with our actions, our promises are kept, and our dealings with others are marked by honesty and fairness. When we commit to a child that we will be somewhere at a certain time, or that we will follow through on a particular consequence, we must do so. Breaking a promise, even a small one, erodes trust and teaches them that words are often cheap. Consider the simple act of returning extra change to a cashier. This may seem insignificant to us, but to a child watching, it's a clear demonstration of honesty. They are learning that what is right is right, regardless of whether anyone is watching. Similarly, when we speak about people, our words should reflect the same love and respect we are teaching them to extend. Gossiping or speaking ill of others, even in hushed tones, contradicts the biblical mandate to love our neighbor. Children will notice this disconnect and learn to emulate it. Living with integrity means being transparent about our mistakes and demonstrating repentance. If we accidentally damage something or say something unkind, owning up to it, apologizing, and seeking to make amends is a powerful lesson in accountability and humility. It teaches them that no one is perfect, but that integrity lies in how we respond to our imperfections.

Kindness, too, is a fruit of the Spirit that is best cultivated through lived example. Our interactions with our spouse, with our children, with neighbors, and even with strangers, are constantly being evaluated by our children. When we go out of our way to help someone, to offer a word of encouragement, or to show compassion to someone in need, we are painting a vivid picture of what it means to love like Jesus. This might be as simple as holding a door open for someone, offering a listening ear to a friend who is struggling, or being patient with a slow driver. These acts, seemingly small, weave together a tapestry of a kind and compassionate heart. If we are quick to anger, impatient with those who inconvenience us, or dismissive of others' needs, our children will learn to adopt these less Christ-like behaviors. They will internalize the message that self-interest and quick temper are acceptable responses. The goal is to create an environment where kindness is the default setting, not an occasional exception.

The practice of forgiveness, both receiving it and extending it, is a profound demonstration of faith. When we have wronged our children, or they have wronged us, the way we navigate the process of reconciliation speaks volumes. A sincere apology, followed by a clear path toward restoration, teaches them the beautiful truth of God's forgiveness and our call to emulate it. If we hold grudges or refuse to forgive easily, we are demonstrating a flawed understanding of the grace we have received. Conversely, when we can extend grace to our children after they have made a mistake, and when we can readily admit our own shortcomings and ask for their forgiveness, we are modeling a living Christianity that is both relatable and aspirational. It teaches them that relationships are built on grace, and that true strength lies in the ability to forgive.

Our commitment to Scripture should be more than just quoting verses; it should be evident in how its truths influence our decisions and shape our perspectives. When facing a dilemma, our children should see us turning to the Word, not just for answers, but for principles that guide our thinking. This might involve discussing a moral issue from a biblical standpoint, using Scripture to comfort or encourage, or simply reading it together as a family. This consistent engagement with God's Word demonstrates its relevance and its authority in our lives. It shows them that the Bible is not an ancient relic, but a living, breathing guide for every aspect of life.

Furthermore, our involvement in the church community, our generosity, and our willingness to serve others are all visible aspects of our faith that impact our children. When they see us prioritizing worship, giving cheerfully to those in need, and actively participating in ministry, they learn that faith is not a private matter but a communal one that extends outward. They learn that the body of Christ is important, and that contributing to its well-being is a joyful responsibility. If our faith is confined to Sunday mornings and our giving is reluctant, our children may come to see faith as a duty rather than a delight.

The very rhythm of our days can be a testament to our faith. The way we manage our time, prioritize our responsibilities, and seek rest and renewal can all reflect a life lived in dependence on God. If we are constantly stressed, overwhelmed, and driven by an insatiable pursuit of worldly success, our children may infer that this is the ultimate goal of life. But if they see us seeking balance, trusting God with our schedules, and finding contentment in Him, they will learn to value spiritual well-being over frantic activity. This modeling of a life of faith and integrity is not about achieving an unattainable standard of perfection, but about embracing authenticity, consistently seeking God's will, and allowing His love to flow through us in all our interactions. It is in this genuine, lived expression of our faith that we effectively lead our children in the ways of the Lord, creating a legacy of belief that is deeply rooted and vibrantly alive.

Authenticity in our faith journey is paramount. Children are incredibly perceptive to hypocrisy. They can discern when our words do not match our deeds, or when our outward profession of faith doesn't align with our inner disposition or our daily habits. This is why the modeling of faith and integrity isn't about performing a flawless act but about living out our faith with genuine vulnerability and a reliance on God's grace. When we stumble, as we inevitably will, how we respond is a powerful teaching moment. Do we hide our failures, pretend they didn't happen, or blame others? Or do we acknowledge our mistakes, seek forgiveness, and demonstrate a commitment to learning and growing? The latter approach, while more challenging, is far more impactful. It teaches our children that faith isn't about being sinless, but about being redeemed and continually transformed by God's love.

Consider the practice of confession and repentance within the family. When a parent admits to a child, "I was wrong to speak to you so sharply. I was impatient, and I need to ask for your forgiveness," they are demonstrating a powerful aspect of integrity. This act not only model's humility but also teaches the child the importance of seeking reconciliation and the restorative nature of confession. It shows them that asking for forgiveness is a sign of strength, not weakness, and that our relationships are paramount. This extends to how we handle disagreements between siblings. Instead of simply imposing a solution, we can guide them through a process of understanding each other's perspectives, admitting fault, and offering apologies. This model's conflict resolution rooted in biblical principles of love and forgiveness.

Our financial stewardship is another area where our faith and integrity are constantly on display. If we are prone to excessive consumerism, debt, or a lack of generosity, our children will learn to adopt similar patterns. Conversely, if they witness us living contentedly within our means, giving cheerfully to God's work and to those in need, and demonstrating a responsible approach to managing resources, they will internalize these values. This doesn't require our children to know the exact details of our finances, but rather to see the outward expressions of our faith through our stewardship. They see us prioritizing giving over hoarding, contentment over covetousness, and generosity over selfishness. This teaches them that our trust is in God, not in material possessions, and that true wealth is found in a life lived according to His principles.

The way we approach our work, and our vocations also speaks volumes about our faith. Do we approach our jobs with diligence and excellence, viewing them as opportunities to serve God and to be a positive influence in the world? Or do we approach them with a spirit of grumbling, laziness, or a sole focus on personal gain? Children observe our attitudes towards our responsibilities and learn to either embrace a work ethic that honors God or to adopt one that is self-serving and lackadaisical. When they see us committed to doing our best, treating colleagues with respect, and striving for integrity in our professional lives, they are learning valuable lessons about diligence, honesty, and the dignity of work. Even if our work is not directly related to ministry, it can still be a powerful platform for demonstrating our faith.

Furthermore, our consistent effort to cultivate inner qualities such as patience, self-control, and gratitude is crucial. These are not always outwardly visible in the same way as an act of kindness, but they are woven into the fabric of our daily interactions. When we respond to traffic jams with calm rather than road rage, when we exercise patience with a fussy baby, or when we consistently express gratitude for the blessings in our lives, our children are absorbing these attitudes. They learn that inner peace and joy are cultivated through dependence on God and a conscious effort to align our hearts with His. This modeling of internal character development is vital, as it equips our children with the tools to develop these same qualities in their own lives.

The modeling of faith and integrity is an ongoing process, not a one-time event. It requires intentionality, self-awareness, and a deep reliance on the Holy Spirit to guide us. It means regularly examining our own hearts and motivations, ensuring that our actions are consistent with our beliefs, and being willing to learn and grow. Children are not passive recipients of our teachings; they are active participants in our spiritual journey. By living out our faith authentically, we are not only guiding them in the ways of the Lord but also inviting them to join us on that path, creating a shared journey of faith that strengthens our bonds and deepens our understanding of God's love for us all. It is through this consistent, unwavering, and grace-filled modeling that we build a spiritual legacy that will endure.

Chapter 5: Daily Rhythms of Faith and Family

Establishing a God-centered morning routine is not about achieving perfection but about prioritizing intentionality. In the beautiful, yet often chaotic, dance of family life, the morning hours can easily become a blur of demands – feeding hungry mouths, coordinating school preparations, and managing the ever-present to-do list. However, by intentionally carving out space for spiritual connection before the world rushes in, we can transform our mornings from a source of stress into a wellspring of peace and purpose for ourselves and, by extension, our families. This isn't about adding another item to an already overflowing plate; it's about reordering priorities, placing our anchor firmly in God before the waves of daily life begin to crash. The goal is to begin the day grounded in His presence, allowing His truth and His peace to permeate our thoughts, our attitudes, and our interactions.

The bedrock of a God-centered morning is quiet time. This is a sacred appointment with the Creator, a moment to simply be in His presence, unhurried and undistracted. For many, this might mean waking up before the rest of the household stirs. While the initial thought of sacrificing precious sleep might seem daunting, the spiritual dividends are immeasurable. Even fifteen to thirty minutes dedicated to God can recalibrate the soul. This time is not about consuming information; it's about communion. It's a time for silent contemplation, for listening to the gentle whisper of the Holy Spirit, and for offering our hearts and our day to Him. Think of it as tending to the roots of a tree before its branches are buffeted by the wind. When our inner spiritual life is nourished, we are far better equipped to weather the storms that the day may bring. This sacred pause can involve reading a passage of Scripture, but it's equally vital to simply rest in God's love, to acknowledge His sovereignty, and to offer Him our gratitude for the gift of a new day. It's about setting a spiritual intention for the hours ahead, aligning our will with His.

Personal prayer is another non-negotiable element of this

intentional start. This is our direct line to the Father, a time to pour out our hearts, confess our shortcomings, and intercede for our loved ones. Begin by acknowledging God's faithfulness. Thank Him for waking you, for the breath in your lungs, for the roof over your head, and for the family He has entrusted to you. Then, bring your concerns before Him. Pray for wisdom in decision-making, for patience in challenging moments, and for opportunities to be His hands and feet. Specifically, lift your children and spouse to God. Pray for their protection, their spiritual growth, their relationships, and for them to know God's love in a deep and personal way. Consider dedicating specific days to praying for particular family members or specific needs. This focused prayer can feel more tangible and impactful. It's also a powerful practice to pray for your own character – for increased faith, for greater love, for a spirit of humility and self-control. Remember, prayer isn't a monologue; it's a dialogue. Be willing to listen for God's direction and comfort through His Word and the quiet promptings of the Spirit. This consistent act of bringing our requests to God cultivates dependence on Him, transforming anxiety into assurance and confusion into clarity.

Engaging with Scripture, even briefly, is essential for grounding our thoughts in God's truth. The Bible is our spiritual nourishment, offering guidance, correction, and encouragement. For those struggling to find time, consider a devotional that is concise yet rich in meaning. Many excellent resources offer short readings designed for busy lives. Alternatively, choose a psalm or a proverb that resonates with your needs for the day. The key is not to read a large quantity but to meditate on a small portion, allowing its truth to sink into your heart. Ask yourself: What is God teaching me through this passage? How can I apply this truth to my day? This focused engagement helps to internalize God's Word, making it a living and active part of your thought process. It's like planting seeds in fertile soil; the results may not be immediate, but with consistent watering through meditation and prayer, they will yield a harvest of transformed thinking and behavior. Even a few verses, truly absorbed, can shift your perspective and equip you to face the day with a spiritual resilience that transcends circumstance.

A peaceful, faith-filled start can indeed set a positive tone for the entire family. When we approach the morning with a sense of calm and reliance on God, this tranquility tends to permeate the atmosphere. Children are highly attuned to their parents' emotional states. If we start the day frazzled and stressed, they will pick up on that energy. Conversely, if they see us entering the day with a quiet confidence rooted in our faith, this can create a ripple effect of peace throughout the household. It models for them that even amidst the busyness, there is a source of strength and serenity available. This doesn't mean the morning will be devoid of challenges, but it means our *response* to those challenges can be different. It's about cultivating an internal stillness that allows us to navigate the inevitable disruptions with grace.

Consider the practicalities of implementing such a routine. It requires discipline and commitment, but also flexibility. Life with children is unpredictable, and there will be days when your carefully planned quiet time is interrupted. On those mornings, don't despair. Simply do what you can. Perhaps it's a five-minute prayer while making coffee, or a quick scan of a verse on your phone before stepping out the door. The intention matters. God sees your heart and your effort to prioritize Him. It's also beneficial to communicate the importance of this time to your spouse and, as your children grow, to involve them in age-appropriate ways. You might read a short devotional together after breakfast or have a family prayer time before the day's activities commence.

The impact of a God-centered morning routine extends beyond the individual. It creates a spiritual anchor for the entire family. When children witness their parents consistently seeking God, they learn that faith is not merely an inherited belief system but a lived reality, a vital lifeline. This modeling instills in them the understanding that God is accessible, that He cares, and that seeking His wisdom is the most sensible first step in any endeavor. It cultivates a spiritual maturity that will serve them throughout their lives, equipping them to face their own challenges with faith rather than fear. This intentional start to the day is an investment in the spiritual well-being of your home, a declaration that God is indeed the cornerstone of your family. It's a daily recommitment to a life lived in His presence, a conscious effort to allow His love and truth to shape the beginning of each day, and consequently, the trajectory of your family's spiritual journey. The quiet moments we steal for God in the morning are not lost time; they are the most productive hours of our day, laying the foundation for all that is to come. This proactive spiritual engagement builds resilience within us, enabling us to parent from a place of spiritual fullness rather than depletion.

Furthermore, a well-established morning routine, centered on faith, can foster a greater sense of order and predictability within the home. While spontaneity is valuable, a consistent structure can reduce morning chaos, especially for children who thrive on routine. Knowing what to expect – a quiet moment for Mom or Dad, a shared prayer, a brief scripture reading – can create a sense of security and calm. This predictability doesn't stifle joy; rather, it provides a stable framework within which joy can flourish. It also teaches children the value of discipline and commitment, demonstrating that setting aside time for important matters, even when it requires effort, is a worthwhile endeavor. This foundational understanding of discipline, rooted in spiritual priority, can then be applied to other areas of their lives, from academic pursuits to character development.

The essence of a God-centered morning is about intentionality. It's about consciously choosing to align our lives with His will from the very first moments of the day. This might involve a few moments of silent reflection, recalling the blessings of the past day and offering gratitude for the opportunities of the present. It could be listening to a worship song that lifts your spirit or reading a short devotional that offers a fresh perspective. The specific activities are less important than the underlying intention: to honor God and to draw strength from His presence. When we approach the morning with this mindset, we are less likely to be swept away by the current of daily demands. Instead, we can stand firm in our faith, allowing God to guide our steps and shape our responses.

Consider the practical application for families with very young children. While a lengthy quiet time might seem impossible, even a few minutes of prayer while holding your baby or singing a worship song with your toddler can set a spiritual tone. These small acts, consistently performed, speak volumes. As children grow, you can adapt the routine to include them. Perhaps a shared family prayer circle before breakfast, or a short Bible story read aloud. The goal is to integrate faith into the fabric of everyday life, and the morning is a prime opportunity to do so. These shared spiritual moments build family connection and instill a shared understanding of God's place in your home. It's about creating a spiritual legacy, one morning at a time.

The quiet commitment to seeking God's face in the morning is a powerful statement to your children about what truly matters. It demonstrates that your relationship with the Lord is not an afterthought but a priority. This consistent practice cultivates in them an understanding that spiritual nourishment is as essential as physical nourishment. It teaches them that God is not a distant entity to be acknowledged only on Sundays, but a present Father with whom they can have a personal relationship. This early exposure to consistent, faith-filled habits can shape their own spiritual trajectories in profound ways, laying a foundation for a lifetime of seeking and knowing God. The intentionality behind these mornings is an investment in eternity, a tangible expression of your love for God and your desire to lead your family in His ways. It is in these quiet, sacred moments that the strength and wisdom needed for the day ahead are found, a testament to the power of beginning with God. This disciplined approach to spiritual intake is not a burden but a privilege, an opportunity to be filled with God's presence before being poured out into the demands of family life. It cultivates a spiritual resilience that allows us to face challenges not from a place of depletion, but from a place of divine replenishment, ensuring that our family life is anchored in the unshakable truth of God's Word and His unwavering love.

The morning has set the spiritual tone, but the demands of family life rarely conclude with the breakfast dishes. As the hours of the day unfold, filled with the rhythm of meals, learning, play, and household management, it's easy for our focus to drift, for the spiritual anchor we established to loosen its grip. Yet, it is precisely in the midst of these midday activities that our faith needs to be not just a starting point, but a sustaining force. We must actively seek out and cultivate "Midday Moments" where we can intentionally reconnect with God, drawing fresh strength and perspective to navigate the hours ahead. These aren't grand, scheduled events, but rather small, deliberate pauses that allow us to remain in communion with our Heavenly Father, even while our hands are busy, or our minds are occupied with the practicalities of homemaking and family care.

One of the most accessible ways to weave faith into the fabric of the midday is through short, focused prayer breaks. These are not lengthy, eloquent petitions, but rather fleeting, heartfelt conversations with God that can be incorporated into the natural flow of our day. Think of them as spiritual pit stops, quick moments to refuel and reorient. While folding laundry, you might pause for a silent prayer of gratitude for the provision of clothing and the family who wears it. While preparing lunch, you could offer a brief prayer for wisdom and patience as you nourish your children, asking for guidance in shaping their minds and hearts through the simple act of feeding them. Even while engaged in cleaning, a quick mental invocation – "Lord, help me to see this as an act of service to my family and to You" – can transform a mundane chore into an act of worship. These moments can be as simple as closing your eyes for thirty seconds while standing at the kitchen sink, or as you walk from one room to another, whispering a single word of praise or a request for help. The key is intentionality; it's about consciously turning your heart and mind towards God, even amidst the most ordinary tasks. Consider setting a gentle reminder on your phone, perhaps a word like "Jesus" or "Trust," that prompts you to pause and reconnect. These brief interludes, repeated throughout the day, create a continuous thread of spiritual awareness, preventing the world's distractions from completely overshadowing your connection with God. It's akin to a gardener regularly watering young plants; these consistent, small applications of spiritual discipline ensure that our inner lives remain vibrant and nourished, rather than wilting under the heat of daily pressures. The cumulative effect of these midday prayers is profound, fostering a deeper sense of God's presence in our lives and cultivating a spirit of reliance on Him throughout the entirety of our day, not just at its beginning.

Beyond spoken prayer, mindful reflection on Scripture can also serve as a powerful midday nourishment. We don't always have the luxury of leisurely Bible study during the day, but we can carry the essence of God's Word with us. Perhaps you've read a particularly impactful verse or passage in the morning; throughout the day, recall those words. As you are tidying up after a meal, bring to mind a verse about contentment or serving others. While watching your children play, meditate on a psalm that speaks of God's love and protection. You can even utilize technology to your advantage. Many apps offer daily verses or short devotional thoughts that can be accessed quickly. Carry a small, pocket-sized Bible or a devotional booklet with you. When you find yourself with a spare moment – perhaps while waiting for an appointment, or during a child's naptime – open it to a random page and allow the Holy Spirit to highlight a truth for you. This isn't about checking a box but about allowing God's Word to actively engage your thoughts, to shape your perspective, and to infuse your spirit with His truth. Consider the practice of scripture memorization. Even memorizing a single verse can provide a powerful internal resource. When stress levels rise, or you feel overwhelmed, recalling that verse can be an instant anchor, a reminder of God's promises and His faithfulness. For instance, if you're struggling with impatience, memorizing Philippians 4:6, "Do not be anxious about anything, but in every situation, by prayer and petition, with thanksgiving, present your requests to God," can be a

119

lifeline. You can mentally recite this verse as you feel frustration building, consciously choosing to hand your anxieties over to Him. This internal engagement with scripture transforms passive reception into active application, making God's Word a living, breathing force in your daily life.

The modern age has also gifted us with incredible resources for spiritual growth that can be seamlessly integrated into our busy days. Consider the power of Christian podcasts or audiobooks. While you are engaged in physical tasks that don't require intense mental focus, such as washing dishes, vacuuming, or even going for a walk, you can be spiritually edified. There are countless podcasts available that offer insightful biblical teaching, encouraging testimonies, and practical advice for living a faith-filled life. This allows you to multitask in a spiritually productive way. Instead of listening to secular music or talk radio, choose content that uplifts, challenges, and inspires you. This exposure to sound biblical teaching can reinforce the truths you encountered in your morning quiet time and provide new perspectives for navigating the challenges of the day. It's like having a wise spiritual mentor available to you at any moment. Many of these podcasts are designed for busy listeners, offering episodes that are ten to thirty minutes long, making them perfect for fitting into a packed schedule. You can subscribe to several and rotate through them based on your needs or interests for the day. For example, on a day when you feel particularly discouraged, you might choose a podcast focused on overcoming adversity, or on a day when you're wrestling with a specific parenting challenge, you might seek out one that offers biblical counsel on raising children. The accessibility of this content means that spiritual growth is no longer confined to specific times or locations; it can happen wherever you are, and whatever you are doing, as long as you make the intentional choice to tune in. This deliberate selection of audio content is a powerful way to curate your spiritual environment, ensuring that the messages you absorb are nurturing your faith rather than depleting it.

Furthermore, cultivating an attitude of worship throughout the day can transform ordinary moments into opportunities for spiritual connection. Worship isn't solely reserved for Sunday mornings or dedicated worship services. It's a posture of the heart that acknowledges God's worth and expresses our love and devotion to Him. This can manifest in various ways during the midday. Perhaps as you are tidying up your home, you sing a hymn or a contemporary worship song under your breath. Even if your voice isn't perfect, God hears the heart behind the song. The simple act of singing praises can lift your spirits and remind you of God's goodness and sovereignty. You might also engage in acts of service that are offered as worship to God. When you respond with grace to a difficult request from a child, or patiently explain something for the tenth time, you are honoring God through your actions. The Apostle Paul encourages us in Romans 12:1 to "present your bodies as a living sacrifice, holy and acceptable to God, which is your spiritual worship." This means that every aspect of our lives, including our midday activities, can be an act of worship when offered with the right intention. Consider how you can intentionally offer your tasks as worship. When you are preparing a meal, you can pray, "Lord, thank you for this food, and I offer this preparation as a sacrifice of praise to you." When you are cleaning, you can see it as an act of stewardship over the home God has provided. This shift in perspective elevates the mundane, infusing it with divine purpose and transforming it into an opportunity for spiritual engagement. The practice of gratitude is another vital element of sustaining faith through the midday. It's easy to get caught up in the pressures and demands of the day, focusing on what's wrong or what still needs to be done. However, deliberately pausing to acknowledge what we are thankful for can dramatically shift our perspective and strengthen our faith. During the hustle and bustle of lunchtime or afternoon chores, take a moment to identify three things you are grateful for. It could be the warmth of the sun on your skin, the laughter of your children, a successful task completed, or simply the ability to breathe and function. Writing these down in a journal, even a simple note on your phone, can be a powerful practice. This exercise in gratitude cultivates a heart that recognizes God's continuous provision and faithfulness, even in the midst of challenges. It combats the spirit of complaint and entitlement that can easily creep in when we are feeling overwhelmed. Think of it as an antidote to discontentment. When we actively seek out the blessings, however small, we train our hearts to see God's hand at work in every circumstance. This intentional focus on gratitude can transform your emotional landscape, replacing anxiety with peace and frustration with thankfulness. It's a way of actively participating in the joy of the Lord, recognizing that joy is not dependent on circumstances but on our connection to Him.

Another practical approach to integrating faith into the midday is to create "sacred spaces" within your home. These don't need to be elaborate or formal. It could be a comfortable chair in a quiet corner where you intentionally sit for a few minutes with your Bible and a cup of tea. It might be a beautifully arranged shelf with a cross, a devotional book, and a picture of your family, serving as a visual reminder of your spiritual priorities. Even a small vase of flowers placed where you'll see it frequently can serve as a prompt to pause and offer a moment of reflection or prayer. The purpose of these spaces is to provide a tangible cue, an anchor point in your day, that draws you back to God. When you pass by that designated spot, or settle into that chair, it's a signal to your mind and spirit to reconnect. These intentional markers help to break the spell of distraction and bring you back into a conscious awareness of God's presence. Consider where you spend the most time during the day. Can you create a small sacred space in that area? Perhaps it's near the kitchen sink, or in the living room where the children often play. The key is to make it accessible and inviting, a place where you can easily steal a few moments for spiritual refreshment.

Furthermore, family interaction, even during the midday, presents opportunities to model and share your faith. While the morning routine might focus on individual spiritual intake, the midday can offer more integrated family faith moments. For example, during lunch, you could share a brief testimony of how God helped you with something that day or ask each family member to share something they are thankful for. Even simple mealtime prayers can be opportunities for deeper connection. Instead of a rote prayer, encourage each person to add a specific word of thanks or a particular prayer request. As children grow, they can be given opportunities to lead prayer. This not only reinforces their understanding of prayer but also empowers them to take an active role in the spiritual life of the family. Another approach is to incorporate short, faith-based activities during transition times. For instance, while waiting for lunch to finish cooking, you might read a short Bible story or a chapter from a Christian children's book. These brief, shared spiritual experiences create a sense of unity and reinforce the message that faith is an integral part of your family's life, woven into the fabric of everyday moments. It's about intentionally creating these touchpoints that remind everyone, including yourself, that God is at the center of your home, not just during scheduled devotions, but throughout the entire day.

The midday can also be a time to consciously practice spiritual disciplines that build resilience. For instance, the practice of "recollection" – a brief, focused mental review of your actions and thoughts to ensure they align with God's will – can be incredibly beneficial. Throughout the day, take moments to ask yourself: "Where has God been with me in the last hour? What were my dominant thoughts and feelings? Did my actions reflect my commitment to Christ?" This self-examination, done with gentleness and honesty, can help you identify areas where you may have drifted and bring them back into alignment. It's not about self-condemnation, but about a loving awareness of your spiritual state and a conscious redirection towards God. This practice, similar to a quick check of the rearview mirror while driving, ensures you're staying on the right path. Another discipline that can sustain faith is the conscious effort to see people and situations through God's eyes. When you encounter someone who is difficult, or a situation that is frustrating, try to remember that God loves that person just as much as He loves you. Pray for that person, asking God to reveal His heart towards them. This shift from personal offense to intercession can diffuse anger and cultivate compassion, transforming potentially negative interactions into opportunities for spiritual growth. It's a testament to the transformative power of extending God's grace, starting with yourself and extending outward.

Ultimately, these Midday Moments are about cultivating a dynamic, active faith that doesn't get put away with the morning devotionals. They are about remembering that God is with us, in the quiet and in the chaos, and that He desires to be in relationship with us throughout the entire day. By intentionally weaving prayer, scripture reflection, worship, gratitude, and mindful presence into the fabric of our midday, we create a sustained connection with God that nourishes our souls, strengthens our families, and allows us to navigate the complexities of life with His enduring peace and perspective. These are not extra burdens to bear, but life-giving opportunities to remain anchored in Him, ensuring that our spiritual journey is not confined to a single point in the day, but is a continuous, vibrant stream of connection with our Creator. This consistent engagement with the divine acts as a spiritual thermostat, regulating our inner climate and ensuring that even when the external pressures rise, our internal connection to God remains steadfast and warm.

The conclusion of a day, much like its beginning, holds significant spiritual potential for our families. As the sun dips below the horizon and the demands of daytime activities begin to wane, a unique opportunity arises to cultivate a transition from busyness to blessed stillness. This "Evening Wind-Down" is not merely about preparing bodies for sleep, but more importantly, about preparing hearts for rest, for communion with God, and for the anticipation of a new day renewed in His strength. It's in these twilight hours that we can gently guide our children, and ourselves, into a space of reflection, gratitude, and peace, grounded in our faith. The aim is to create a sanctuary of calm, a deliberate counterpoint to the inevitable hurriedness of modern life, ensuring that our final hours awake are spent fostering spiritual connection and acknowledging the Lord's faithfulness.

One of the most cherished and impactful ways to usher in this evening calm is through the tradition of reading bedtime stories. However, to align with our goal of daily spiritual rhythm, these stories can be chosen with intentionality. Instead of selecting any captivating tale, we can opt for narratives that gently weave in themes of faith, virtue, and God's love. Think of the classic stories that impart moral lessons, but elevate them by choosing those that explicitly point to God's presence, His sovereignty, or His character. Many Christian authors have beautifully crafted stories that explore biblical principles in accessible language for children. These might be tales about characters who demonstrate courage through faith, practice kindness because of God's example, or learn to trust Him through challenging circumstances. Even seemingly secular stories can be opportunities for discussion, drawing out the underlying values and asking questions like, "How did that character show God's love?" or "What can we learn about God from this character's actions?" The act of reading aloud itself is a profound bonding experience. As we sit with our children, our voices soft and comforting, the words we choose become seeds planted in their hearts. It's a time to slow down, to snuggle close, and to create a warm, secure environment where spiritual truths can be absorbed naturally. The physical closeness, the shared focus on the words and illustrations, and the calm tone all contribute to a sense of peace that can calm even the most energetic child. This ritual, repeated night after night, builds a strong association between bedtime, comfort, and spiritual nourishment. It's a tangible expression of our desire to impart our faith not as a set of rules, but as a living, breathing reality that shapes our lives and brings us joy.

Beyond the narrative of a book, shared family prayer is a cornerstone of the evening wind-down. This is a sacred time to collectively turn our hearts towards God, acknowledging His goodness and entrusting our families to His care throughout the night. It's an opportunity to teach children the power and practice of prayer, moving beyond rote recitations to a more personal and heartfelt engagement. Instead of a generic "Amen," encourage each family member to share something they are thankful for from the day. This simple practice cultivates a spirit of gratitude, reinforcing the principle of giving thanks in all circumstances. It might be a child thanking God for a fun afternoon with a friend, a spouse expressing gratitude for a particular act of kindness, or yourself acknowledging God's strength in navigating a difficult situation. Furthermore, this is the ideal time to bring our petitions to Him. Encourage the sharing of prayer requests, whether they are personal struggles, concerns for loved ones, or hopes for the future. As parents, we can model vulnerability by sharing our own needs, showing our children that it's okay to rely on God and to ask for His help. This shared vulnerability fosters deeper connection within the family and with God. Consider making prayer time more interactive. For older children, you might invite them to lead a portion of the prayer, perhaps focusing on thanking God for something specific they learned that day, or praying for a particular need within the family. This not only reinforces their understanding of prayer but also empowers them to take ownership of their faith journey. Even younger children can participate by holding hands, closing their eyes, or repeating simple phrases of praise. The key is to make it a consistent, cherished part of your family's rhythm, a predictable anchor in the ebb and flow of daily life.

The practice of discussing the day's blessings, or what is often called a "gratitude review," can powerfully complement both bedtime stories and family prayer. This is not about recounting every minute detail, but about intentionally identifying moments where God's presence, provision, or grace was evident. It's a gentle way to shift focus from what went wrong or what remains unfinished, to what God has done. You might ask open-ended questions like, "What was a highlight of your day?" or "What is something good that happened today?" Encourage specific answers, helping your children to see God's hand even in seemingly small things. Did a friend share a toy? That's God's kindness. Did you finish a challenging assignment? That's God's strength. Did you feel loved and safe? That's God's protection. This practice trains the heart to be attentive to God's work in the everyday, building a reservoir of faith and contentment.

For parents, this reflection can also be an opportunity to affirm your children's good behavior or efforts, connecting their positive actions to God's principles. "I was so proud of how you shared your snacks today. That's a beautiful way to show God's love to others." This reinforces the connection between godly living and personal character. It also provides a natural segue into prayer, as you can then pray specifically for the blessings that were shared. This consistent practice cultivates a deep-seated gratitude that can serve as a powerful antidote to entitlement and dissatisfaction, anchoring your children in the truth that life's true joy comes from recognizing and appreciating God's abundant goodness.

To further enhance this evening wind-down, consider incorporating elements that promote physical and mental calm. This might involve gentle activities that signal to the body and mind that it is time to transition from activity to rest. For instance, dimming the lights in the house an hour or so before bedtime can create a more serene atmosphere. Switching off electronic devices that emit blue light, which can interfere with sleep, is also a wise practice. Instead of screens, families can engage in quiet, screen-free activities. This could include drawing or coloring, simple puzzles, or listening to calming instrumental music or Christian audio dramas. The aim is to gradually lower the sensory input, allowing for a natural descent into a state of relaxation. For younger children, a warm bath can be a wonderfully soothing ritual, perhaps with gentle essential oils like lavender known for their calming properties. For older children and adults, a warm cup of herbal tea can be a comforting pre-sleep beverage. These activities are not just about physical comfort; they are about creating a peaceful environment that is conducive to spiritual reflection and rest. They communicate to the family that this time is dedicated to peace and connection, both with each other and with God. This deliberate creation of a tranquil environment is a tangible expression of love and care, preparing the way for deeper spiritual engagement.

Another vital aspect of the evening wind-down is fostering a spirit of confession and forgiveness. As the day concludes, it's natural for minor conflicts or moments of selfishness to have occurred. Creating a safe space for children (and parents) to acknowledge any wrongdoings, ask for forgiveness, and extend it to others is crucial for emotional and spiritual health. This can be integrated into the family prayer time or be a separate, brief moment. A simple prompt like, "Is there anything you need to say sorry for today?" or "Is there anyone you need to forgive?" can open the door for honest conversation. As parents, we must model this ourselves, admitting our own mistakes and asking for forgiveness from our children and spouse. This demonstrates that no one is perfect, but that God provides a way for us to restore relationships through confession and forgiveness, mirroring the grace He extends to us. When a child apologizes, receiving it with grace and reassurance is paramount. Statements like, "Thank you for saying sorry. I forgive you, and God forgives you too," can be incredibly affirming. Conversely, if a child has been wronged, encouraging them to forgive, while also acknowledging their hurt, teaches them the power of releasing bitterness. This practice helps to clear the emotional slate, allowing everyone to rest with a lighter heart, unburdened by unresolved grievances. It reinforces the biblical principle found in Ephesians 4:32: "Be kind and compassionate to one another, forgiving each other, just as in Christ God forgave you."

The selection of music for the evening hours can also play a significant role in setting a peaceful, faith-filled tone. Opting for instrumental worship music, hymns sung softly, or contemporary worship songs with a contemplative feel can create a calming ambiance. This music should be gentle, not overly stimulating, and should evoke feelings of peace, reverence, and surrender. It serves as a subtle reminder of God's presence and love, permeating the home with a spiritual atmosphere. As you transition from dinner to winding down activities, having this soothing music playing softly in the background can help to naturally draw hearts towards peace. It's a conscious choice to curate the auditory environment of your home, ensuring that the sounds filling your space are edifying and contribute to a sense of spiritual rest. This is a gentle yet powerful way to maintain a connection with God even during routine activities, transforming the ordinary into opportunities for worship.

Moreover, preparing for the next day with a prayerful mindset can be a valuable component of the evening wind-down. While the focus is on resting, it's also beneficial to cast any anxieties about the coming day onto God. This can involve a brief prayer acknowledging the unknowns of tomorrow and asking for God's guidance, strength, and protection. It's a way of handing over the reins, trusting that He is already present and at work in the days to come. This proactive entrustment can alleviate worry and promote a sense of peace that carries into sleep. For children, this might involve praying about specific events they are looking forward to or perhaps apprehensive about. For example, a child might pray about a school test or a playdate. This encourages them to see God as involved in all aspects of their lives, not just the spiritual ones. This practice reinforces the belief that God is a constant companion, present in our past, our present, and our future. It's a declaration of faith in His unfailing faithfulness, a quiet confidence that even before the day begins, God is already there, preparing the way.

Finally, the act of physically preparing for rest—laying out clothes, packing lunches, tidying up common areas—can also be infused with a spiritual dimension. Viewing these tasks not as chores, but as acts of stewardship and preparation for a new day, can transform them. As you prepare, you can silently pray for the day ahead, for your family, and for yourself. This is a practical way to bring faith into the mundane, aligning your actions with your spiritual commitments. It's about approaching these preparatory tasks with a heart of gratitude for the order and opportunity they represent. This meticulous preparation, done with a prayerful spirit, ensures that the morning begins with less frantic rushing and more intentionality, setting a positive tone for the entire day. It's about creating a seamless flow from restful evening to purposeful morning, all under the umbrella of God's watchful care. This holistic approach to the evening wind-down cultivates a family culture where faith is not compartmentalized but is an integrated part of every aspect of life, from bedtime stories to the quiet anticipation of a new dawn.

In the tapestry of a faith-filled home, beyond the rhythm of morning routines and the peace of evening wind-downs, lies the vital thread of intentional family connection. These are the moments we deliberately carve out, the times we guard fiercely against the encroachments of busyness, all with the purpose of nurturing the bonds that tie us together as a family under God. It's about more than just existing in the same space; it's about actively engaging with one another, sharing laughter, navigating challenges, and building a collective story rooted in love and shared faith. These moments are the fertile ground where belonging blossoms, where children feel truly seen and valued, and where spouses reinforce their partnership in building a godly household. Without this intentionality, even the most faith-filled practices can feel like isolated acts, rather than the living expression of a united family committed to Christ.

One of the most accessible and enjoyable avenues for cultivating intentional family connection is through shared activities that foster interaction and create lasting memories. Consider the joy that can erupt from a dedicated family game night. This isn't just about the competition of winning, but about the shared experience of strategy, the bursts of laughter at a silly move, and the gentle camaraderie that builds as you navigate a board or a deck of cards together. The choices are vast, from classic board games that encourage strategic thinking and friendly debate, to cooperative games where the family works as a team against the game itself, fostering a spirit of unity. Even simple card games can provide hours of enjoyment and opportunity for conversation. As you play, observe the dynamics: the thoughtful pauses, the expressions of delight, the shared groans at a bad roll of the dice. These are all windows into your family's hearts, offering insights and opportunities for connection. You might find a quiet child opening up during a game, or a boisterous one learning to temper their excitement. The key is to make it a regular occurrence, a predictable anchor in the week where the world outside fades away, and the focus is solely on the people within your home.

Beyond the confines of the living room, venturing outdoors offers a rich landscape for intentional family time. Nature itself provides a backdrop for shared discovery and adventure, often stripping away distractions and encouraging genuine interaction. Think about a family hike in a local park or a more ambitious trek in a state forest. As you walk, encourage your children to observe the world around them – the intricate patterns on a leaf, the different calls of birds, the sturdy resilience of trees. These moments of shared observation can spark curiosity and lead to deeper conversations about God's creation, His artistry, and His provision for us. A simple picnic lunch amidst the beauty of nature can transform a meal into a special occasion, fostering gratitude for the blessings we enjoy. Even gardening together, planting seeds and nurturing growth, can become a powerful metaphor for spiritual growth within the family, teaching patience, diligence, and the joy of reaping what is sown. These outdoor excursions not only promote physical health but also cultivate a shared appreciation for God's handiwork, creating a sense of wonder and connection to something larger than ourselves.

Perhaps the most profound, yet often overlooked, aspect of intentional family connection is the cultivation of heartfelt conversations. This isn't about interrogations or lectures, but about creating a safe and inviting space where each family member feels heard, understood, and valued. This might happen organically during meals, or it could be initiated through specific prompts. Consider setting aside time for "question of the day" or inviting each person to share a highlight from their week, a challenge they are facing, or something they are grateful for. These conversations are the bedrock of emotional intimacy within a family. As parents, our role is to be active listeners, reflecting what we hear, asking clarifying questions, and offering encouragement and affirmation. It's in these dialogues that we can subtly weave in faith principles, addressing relational issues with biblical wisdom, or celebrating God's faithfulness in specific situations. For example, if a child shares a struggle with a friend, you can discuss biblical principles of conflict resolution or the importance of showing grace. If a spouse shares a victory, you can collectively thank God for His blessings. These aren't just chats; they are opportunities to build understanding, empathy, and a shared spiritual perspective.

Another powerful way to foster intentional connection is through shared creative pursuits. This could involve anything from family art projects, where everyone contributes to a larger canvas, to collaborative storytelling, where each person adds a sentence or a paragraph to build a narrative. Engaging in these activities encourages teamwork, celebrates individual creativity, and provides a tangible outcome of your shared effort. Imagine the satisfaction of creating a family scrapbook, filled with photos and mementos from your adventures and milestones, each entry accompanied by a shared memory or a prayer. Or perhaps it's creating a family song, writing lyrics together that express your faith and your love for one another. These creative endeavors allow each member to contribute their unique gifts and perspectives, reinforcing the idea that everyone has something valuable to offer. They also provide a wonderful way to process emotions, share experiences, and simply enjoy the process of creation together, all within the context of your shared faith.

The spiritual dimension of these intentional connection times is paramount. As you engage in games, outdoor activities, conversations, or creative projects, remember that these are opportunities to anchor your family in Christ. This might involve starting a game night with a short prayer, asking for God's presence and wisdom as you play. During an outdoor adventure, pausing to thank God for the beauty of His creation or to pray for protection and guidance adds a spiritual layer to the experience. In heartfelt conversations, you can offer biblical insights, pray with and for your family members, and model a reliance on God's strength. Even creative projects can be infused with prayer, dedicating your efforts to God and asking Him to bless the time spent together. It's in these integrated moments that faith becomes not just a Sunday affair, but a living, breathing reality that permeates every aspect of family life, strengthening your collective walk with the Lord.

Consider the impact of a "family vision board" session. Gather magazines, craft supplies, and a large poster board, and invite each family member to cut out images and words that represent their dreams, goals, and aspirations for the family, both individually and collectively. As you create this shared visual representation, discuss how these aspirations align with biblical principles and how you can work together, with God's help, to achieve them. This process encourages open communication about hopes and dreams, fosters a sense of shared purpose, and provides a tangible reminder of your family's commitment to building a life that honors God. The act of creating something tangible together, something that reflects your collective journey, is incredibly bonding. It's a visual testament to your unity and your shared commitment to a future guided by faith.

Another highly effective method for fostering intentional connection is through shared service. This could involve volunteering together at a local soup kitchen, participating in a community cleanup event, or simply extending acts of kindness to neighbors. When families serve together, they experience the joy of giving, learn valuable lessons about empathy and compassion, and strengthen their bond through shared purpose. Discussing the impact of your service, reflecting on how it reflects God's love in action, and praying for those you are helping creates a powerful spiritual experience. These acts of service not only benefit others but also forge a deeper connection within the family as you work towards a common, God-honoring goal. It teaches children that their faith is meant to be lived out in the world, not just held within the home.

Remember that the key to intentional family connection is consistency and presence. It's better to have short, regular bursts of quality time than infrequent, drawn-out events that can feel forced. Make it a priority to be fully present during these times, putting away distractions like phones and focusing your attention on your family members. Your engagement, your active listening, and your genuine interest will speak volumes, communicating to your children and spouse that they are your priority. This consistent investment in your relationships builds a foundation of trust and security, creating a family environment where love, faith, and connection can flourish, strengthening the spiritual core of your home. These intentional times are not just about fun; they are about building a legacy of faith and love that will endure for generations.

The practice of gratitude is not merely a pleasant sentiment; it is a profound spiritual discipline, a cornerstone of a life lived in recognition of God's boundless goodness. The Scriptures repeatedly call us to give thanks in all circumstances, a directive that can, at first glance, seem challenging when life's storms rage. Yet, it is precisely in those moments of difficulty that a conscious turning towards thankfulness can become a powerful anchor, shifting our perspective from what is lacking to what is present, from what is broken to what God is still faithfully working. As we cultivate this spirit within our homes, we not only transform our own hearts but also lay a foundation of faith and resilience for our children.

The biblical imperative for gratitude is woven throughout the Old and New Testaments. In the Psalms, we find an outpouring of thanks for God's deliverance, His faithfulness, and His enduring love. Psalm 107:1 exclaims, "Give thanks to the Lord, for he is good; his love endures forever." This isn't a call to a superficial acknowledgment of blessings, but a deep-seated recognition of God's character and His consistent action in our lives. The Apostle Paul, even from the confines of a prison cell, urged the Thessalonians to "give thanks in all circumstances; for this is God's will for you in Christ Jesus" (1

Thessalonians 5:18). This verse is particularly instructive. It doesn't say to give thanks
for all circumstances, which would be impossible and unwise in the face of genuine suffering. Instead, it directs us to give thanks *in* all circumstances. This subtle but crucial distinction empowers us to find reasons for thankfulness amidst hardship, recognizing that God's presence, His promises, and His ultimate victory are always present, even when our immediate circumstances are difficult.

Fostering a culture of thankfulness within the family begins with intentionality, just as we've discussed the importance of intentional family connection. It requires us to actively seek out the blessings that often get overlooked in the hustle of daily life. One of the most accessible and impactful practices is keeping a gratitude journal. This can be as simple as a dedicated notebook or a digital document. The beauty of a journal is its personal nature, allowing each individual to record their thoughts and reflections without pressure. As a mother, I've found immense value in encouraging my children, even from a young age, to jot down or draw one thing they are thankful for each day. For younger ones, it might be a favorite toy, a fun game played with a sibling, or a delicious meal. As they grow, their entries can reflect deeper understanding: a friend's kindness, a teacher's encouragement, a successful test, or a moment of quiet reflection on God's provision. For myself, I've discovered that even on the most trying days, forcing myself to find just one thing – the warmth of the sun, the taste of my morning coffee, a moment of peace – can begin to reorient my spirit.

Beyond individual journals, creating a family gratitude practice can powerfully unite hearts. One method is to designate a time, perhaps during dinner or before bedtime, to go around the table and share something each person is thankful for. This simple act transforms a routine meal into an opportunity for collective reflection and spiritual growth. It's a moment to pause, to consciously acknowledge God's hand in our lives, and to celebrate the good, no matter how small it may seem. Over time, this practice can become a cherished family ritual, a comforting rhythm that reinforces the positive aspects of life and counters the natural tendency to focus on complaints or unmet desires. It teaches children to be observant of God's blessings and to articulate their appreciation, fostering a habit of thanksgiving that will serve them well throughout their lives.

Consider the impact of a "gratitude jar." This is a physical manifestation of thankfulness that can be placed in a prominent spot in the home. Throughout the week, family members can write down their blessings on small slips of paper and deposit them into the jar. On a designated day, perhaps a Sunday evening, the jar can be emptied, and the messages read aloud. This creates a tangible archive of God's faithfulness, a collection of moments that can be revisited during times of discouragement. It's a visual reminder that even when life feels overwhelming, God has been present, providing, protecting, and blessing. This shared act of remembrance can be incredibly fortifying, strengthening the family's collective faith and reminding everyone of the abundance we have received through Christ.

Practicing gratitude has a profound effect on our perspective. When we intentionally look for blessings, we begin to see them everywhere. It's like putting on a new pair of glasses that filter out the negativity and highlight the good. This shift in perspective is not about ignoring difficulties, but about refusing to let them overshadow God's constant presence and provision. When a child is facing a challenging school day, a parent can gently guide them to consider what went well, what they learned, or perhaps a moment of unexpected kindness from a classmate. This doesn't diminish the struggle, but it empowers the child to find strength and hope even in difficult circumstances. Similarly, when we, as adults, are feeling overwhelmed by responsibilities or anxieties, taking a few moments to list the things we are thankful for – our health, our family, the roof over our heads, the salvation we have in Christ – can recalibrate our emotional state. This mental exercise trains our minds to focus on abundance rather than scarcity, on what we have rather than what we lack.

This practice is deeply connected to building resilience. Life inevitably brings trials, disappointments, and losses. A family that cultivates gratitude is better equipped to weather these storms. Gratitude fosters an optimistic outlook, which is a key component of resilience. When faced with adversity, individuals who regularly practice thankfulness are more likely to draw upon their past experiences of God's faithfulness. They have a reservoir of documented blessings to recall, reminding them that God has brought them through difficulties before and will do so again. This creates a sense of hope and a belief in their own capacity, bolstered by faith, to overcome challenges. For children, learning to be thankful amidst setbacks teaches them that difficulties are not the end of the story, but opportunities for growth and for leaning more fully on God. It instills a deep-seated trust in His plan, even when they cannot see the full picture.

Furthermore, gratitude enhances joy. It is a multiplier of happiness. The more we acknowledge and appreciate what we have, the more joy we experience. Conversely, a spirit of entitlement or constant dissatisfaction acts as a joy-killer. By consciously practicing thankfulness, we open ourselves to experiencing a deeper, more profound sense of joy that is not dependent on external circumstances. This joy is rooted in our relationship with God and His unfailing love. When we express thanks, we are acknowledging the source of all good gifts, and this recognition brings a unique and lasting happiness. Imagine the ripple effect in a home where gratitude is a prevailing attitude. Laughter becomes more frequent, interactions are more positive, and the overall atmosphere is one of contentment and peace, a reflection of God's presence.

To truly embed gratitude into the fabric of our daily lives, we must actively look for God's blessings in every circumstance, big or small. This requires a conscious effort to engage our senses and our minds in recognizing His hand. It means being present in the moment and observing the details of our day. Did your child learn a new skill? Thank God for their progress and your role in nurturing them. Did you receive an unexpected kindness from a stranger? Thank God for using that person to brighten your day. Is the weather pleasant, allowing for outdoor activities? Thank God for the beauty of His creation and the opportunity to enjoy it. Even the mundane moments can be infused with thankfulness. The ability to wake up, to breathe, to have a home – these are often taken for granted, but they are profound blessings.

The practice of gratitude also deepens our faith. When we consistently thank God, we are affirming our belief in His sovereignty, His goodness, and His promises. It's an act of worship that acknowledges our dependence on Him and His gracious provision for us. As we observe how God has met our needs, provided for our families, and guided our steps, our trust in Him grows. This strengthens our faith not just as an intellectual assent to truths, but as a living, active trust that impacts our daily decisions and our emotional well-being. When we thank God, we are essentially saying, "I trust You, I believe in You, and I acknowledge Your power and love in my life." This declaration, made repeatedly, transforms our relationship with Him.

To further encourage this practice, consider creating a "Family Blessing Box" alongside the gratitude jar. This could be a more decorative container where specific prayers or answered prayers are written down. When a prayer is answered, instead of just feeling thankful, write it down with a note about the prayer and deposit it in the box. Periodically, you can pull out these notes and read them aloud, reminding yourselves of God's faithfulness in answering prayer. This tangible record serves as a powerful testament to God's active involvement in your family's life, reinforcing the belief that

God hears and responds to the prayers of His people. It's a wonderful way to combat doubt and to strengthen the family's corporate prayer life.

Another practical way to foster gratitude is through acts of service inspired by thankfulness. When we are overwhelmed by God's blessings, it naturally leads to a desire to share that abundance with others. Organize family service projects that are rooted in gratitude. For instance, if you are particularly thankful for the food on your table, consider volunteering at a food bank or preparing meals for a family in need. If you are grateful for the comfort of your home, perhaps you could help with a project for a local shelter. When children participate in these activities, they learn that gratitude is not just about receiving, but also about giving. They see firsthand how their blessings can be a source of blessing to others, and this connects their thankfulness to a tangible expression of God's love in the world.

It is also beneficial to intentionally discuss biblical narratives that highlight gratitude. Read stories of people who expressed profound thanks, like Hannah dedicating Samuel to the Lord or David's Psalms of praise. Discuss how these individuals' thankfulness impacted their lives and their relationship with God. Encourage your children to identify with these characters and to consider how they can emulate their grateful spirit. This helps them understand that gratitude is a theme that runs throughout Scripture, a vital aspect of living a life pleasing to God.

For parents, modeling gratitude is perhaps the most potent tool. Children are keen observers. If they hear you complaining, focusing on what you lack, or expressing dissatisfaction, they will internalize those attitudes. Conversely, if they witness you regularly expressing thanks – for the meal, for their efforts, for a quiet moment, for your spouse – they will learn that this is the natural and appropriate response to life. Verbalize your thankfulness often. Thank your spouse for their contributions to the home and family. Thank your children for their help, their good behavior, or even for just being themselves. These small, spoken words of appreciation reinforce the value you place on them and on the blessings of your family life.

The spiritual discipline of gratitude is not about pretending everything is perfect. It is about choosing to focus on God's faithfulness and goodness, even when circumstances are difficult. It is about recognizing that every good gift comes from Him and that His presence is a reason for thanksgiving. By intentionally incorporating practices like journaling, sharing blessings, and serving others, we can cultivate a spirit of profound gratitude within our families. This practice not only deepens our individual faith and resilience but also creates a home environment filled with joy, peace, and an unwavering awareness of God's abundant love. As we consistently thank Him, we draw closer to the Source of all goodness, experiencing a richer and more fulfilling life of faith. It is a discipline that transforms hearts, strengthens bonds, and ultimately glorifies God.

Chapter 6: Weekly Spiritual Practices for the Family

The seventh day of the week, set apart by God Himself in the very act of creation, carries a profound and often understated significance for the Christian family. It is the Sabbath, a sacred gift intended not as a burden, but as a balm for our weary souls and a cornerstone of our spiritual lives. In a world that relentlessly pulls us in a thousand directions, demanding constant productivity and attention, the Sabbath stands as a divine invitation to pause, to remember, and to reconnect. It is a day of rest, yes, but it is also a day of worship, of fellowship, and of focused spiritual engagement, designed to refresh and strengthen us for the week ahead. Far from being a relic of a bygone era, the Sabbath is a timeless principle, a weekly reset button that, when intentionally honored, can transform our family's spiritual health and deepen our connection with our Creator.

The foundation of the Sabbath is laid in the very first book of the Bible, in Genesis, where we read that on the seventh day, God rested from all His work. He blessed the seventh day and made it holy, because He rested from all the work of creating that He had done (Genesis 2:2-3). This act of divine ceasing is not an indication of weakness or exhaustion on God's part, but rather a deliberate demarcation, a declaration that creation was complete and good. By observing the Sabbath, we participate in this foundational rhythm of God's work and rest, acknowledging His sovereignty over all things and His perfect completion of His creative purpose. This is not just a historical footnote; it is a profound theological statement about the nature of God and His ordered universe.

Jesus Himself affirmed the Sabbath's enduring purpose when He said, "The Sabbath was made for man, not man for the Sabbath" (Mark 2:27). This statement is crucial. It clarifies that the Sabbath is a provision for our well-being, a gift designed to meet our needs for rest and spiritual renewal. It is not an arbitrary rule imposed to control or restrict, but a loving ordinance intended to benefit us. In the midst of His own demanding ministry, Jesus frequently withdrew to pray and rest, demonstrating the importance of periodic cessation from labor. He challenged the rigid and legalistic interpretations of the Sabbath that had become prevalent, emphasizing its restorative and life-affirming qualities. He showed that acts of mercy and care for the needy were not violations of the Sabbath but were, in fact, in keeping with its spirit.

For families in the modern age, observing the Sabbath faithfully requires conscious intention and a willingness to push back against the pervasive culture of constant activity. It means making a deliberate choice to set aside the usual demands of work, chores, and entertainment for a dedicated period of spiritual focus and physical rest. This isn't about creating a day of rigid, joyless rules, but about creating an atmosphere of sacred stillness and intentional engagement with God and with each other. It's about recognizing that this one day in seven is different, set apart for a higher purpose that nourishes the soul.

A vital aspect of preparing for the Sabbath begins on the preceding day, often referred to as Preparation Day. This involves completing as many secular tasks as possible before the sun sets on Saturday evening. This might mean doing laundry, preparing meals in advance, tidying the house, and ensuring all work-related obligations are met. The goal is to minimize the need for "necessary" tasks on the Sabbath itself, allowing for uninterrupted rest and worship. It's a practical way to honor the spirit of the day, creating a clear distinction between the work week and the holy day. Thinking ahead, perhaps on Friday evening or Saturday morning, about what meals can be prepared or partially prepared, or what essential tasks need to be completed, can make the transition into the Sabbath much smoother and more peaceful. This preparation isn't about striving for perfection, but about making a thoughtful effort to enter the Sabbath unburdened by preventable obligations.

One of the most beautiful facets of Sabbath observance is the emphasis on rest. This is not mere idleness, but a deliberate cessation from strenuous or demanding labor. For a mother, this might mean handing over certain responsibilities to her spouse or older children, or simply accepting that not every task needs to be completed on this day. It's about finding ways to truly rest, both physically and mentally. This could involve reading, napping, going for a quiet walk, or engaging in gentle, enjoyable activities that do not feel like work. For children, it means providing opportunities for unstructured play and quiet reflection, away from the demands of screens and organized activities. The key is to create an environment where the family can truly decompress and find respite.

Worship is another central pillar of the Sabbath. This can take many forms, both corporate and personal. Attending a church service is a primary way many families engage in communal worship. However, the Sabbath is also an opportunity to foster worship within the home. This could include a dedicated family worship time, perhaps reading Scripture together, singing hymns or worship songs, and praying. Even simple acts like reading devotional literature or discussing a relevant Bible passage can transform ordinary moments into acts of worship. The focus is on directing our hearts and minds towards God, acknowledging His presence and His goodness in our lives. This could involve creating a special space in the home for family worship, perhaps with a Bible, a devotional book, and candles, to signal that this time is set apart.

Fellowship also plays a significant role in a fulfilling Sabbath. This can involve spending quality time with other believers, perhaps sharing a meal with friends from church or engaging in spiritual conversations. Within the family itself, the Sabbath is an ideal time to deepen bonds. It's a chance to truly connect, free from the distractions of the week. This might mean engaging in board games, having extended conversations, or simply enjoying each other's company without the pressure of a schedule. The emphasis is on building relationships, both with God and with one another. For instance, a family might plan a special Sabbath meal together, where everyone contributes in some small way, and then dedicate time afterward to simply talking and sharing about their week.

Making the Sabbath a blessing also means being mindful of what we bring into this sacred day. While rest is paramount, it doesn't mean complete inactivity. It's about engaging in activities that are life-giving and spiritually nourishing. This might include reading good books, listening to uplifting music, engaging in creative pursuits like drawing or painting, or spending time in nature. The key is to discern what truly refreshes the soul and honors God. For children, this might involve nature walks, imaginative play, or engaging with age-appropriate Christian literature. The goal is to create a rhythm that is both restful and spiritually enriching.

For families, establishing consistent Sabbath practices can be challenging in our fast-paced world. It requires a commitment to setting boundaries and prioritizing this sacred time. It means saying "no" to activities that encroach on the Sabbath and "yes" to those that honor it. It also means being flexible and understanding, recognizing that there will be times when disruptions occur. The important thing is to have a framework in place that allows for consistent observance and to continually seek God's wisdom in how to best honor His day.

One practical approach to enriching family Sabbath time is to designate specific themes or activities for each week. Perhaps one Sabbath could focus on prayer, with dedicated time for each family member to pray for specific needs. Another might center on Scripture memorization, with the family working together to learn a new passage. Yet another could involve acts of kindness, where the family discusses ways to serve others in their community, reflecting the spirit of Jesus' ministry. These themed Sabbaths can add variety and depth to the observance, ensuring that it remains engaging and spiritually formative.

Consider the impact of unplugging from technology. In our digitally saturated lives, the Sabbath offers a much-needed respite from screens. Designating the Sabbath as a "tech-free" day, or at least significantly limiting screen time, can open up space for deeper connection and presence. This allows families to engage with each other and with God without the constant interruptions and distractions of notifications, social media, and entertainment streams. This isn't about demonizing technology, but about recognizing its potential to fragment our attention and detract from the sacredness of the Sabbath.

Another helpful practice is to create a Sabbath box or basket. This can be filled with items that facilitate Sabbath observance: a Bible, devotional books, journals, art supplies for creative expression, or even simple games. Having these resources readily available can make it easier to transition into Sabbath mode and to engage in enriching activities. It becomes a tangible symbol of the day's purpose.

The act of remembrance is also central to the Sabbath. It is a day to remember God's creation, His deliverance of Israel from Egypt, and His ongoing work in our lives. This remembrance can be fostered through storytelling, reading biblical accounts, and reflecting on personal experiences of God's faithfulness. For children, hearing stories of God's mighty acts, whether from Scripture or from family history, can instill a deep appreciation for His power and love.

The Sabbath is not merely a day to avoid work; it is a day to engage in activities that are inherently good and God-honoring. This includes activities that promote spiritual growth, family bonding, and community engagement. It is a day to intentionally seek God's presence and to experience His peace. When we honor the Sabbath, we are not just following a commandment; we are embracing a gift that has the power to refresh, renew, and strengthen our families in profound ways. It is a weekly invitation to enter into God's rhythm of rest and worship, a practice that can profoundly impact our spiritual journey.

The preparation for the Sabbath is an act of love and intentionality. It's about clearing the decks, so to speak, to allow for a sacred space to open. This might involve a family conversation on Friday evening about how to best prepare. Perhaps one parent takes on the responsibility of ensuring meals are ready, while the other tidies the living spaces. Children can be involved in age-appropriate ways, like setting the table for the Sabbath meal or gathering books for family worship. This shared responsibility fosters a sense of collective ownership over the Sabbath, making it a true family affair.

The concept of "holy rest" is something to truly ponder. It's not about being lazy, but about ceasing from labor that exhausts the soul and engaging instead in activities that replenish it. This could mean taking a nap, enjoying a leisurely walk in nature, or simply sitting in quiet contemplation, listening for the still, small voice of God. For children, this might translate to supervised playtime that encourages imagination rather than competition, or quiet reading time with engaging stories. The key is to shift from the demands of the week to a posture of receptivity and peace.

When it comes to family worship on the Sabbath, creativity can be a wonderful asset. It doesn't have to be a formal sermon. It could be a time of singing choruses together, with everyone choosing a song they love. It could involve reading a chapter from a book of Psalms and discussing its message. Or it could be a time for each family member to share something they are thankful for, as we discussed in our chapter on gratitude. The goal is to make it engaging and relevant to the lives of each family member, fostering a shared experience of encountering God.

The Sabbath also provides a wonderful opportunity to extend hospitality. Sharing a Sabbath meal with another family, or inviting someone who might be lonely to join your family worship, can be a powerful expression of God's love. This act of extending our Sabbath blessing to others deepens our own understanding of grace and generosity, reflecting God's abundant provision for us. This could be a regular practice, perhaps inviting a different family or individual each week, or it could be a spontaneous act of kindness when an opportunity arises.

The spiritual discipline of Sabbath observance is an ongoing journey. It requires constant evaluation and adjustment as families grow and circumstances change. What works for a family with young children might need to be adapted as those children become teenagers. The key is to remain committed to the principle of setting aside this day for God, for rest, and for spiritual nourishment. It is a practice that, when embraced with intention and faith, can become a profound blessing to the entire family, drawing you closer to God and to one another week after week. By consistently honoring this sacred rhythm, families can cultivate a deeper spiritual life, a stronger sense of unity, and a more profound appreciation for the gift of God's presence in their lives. This intentionality transforms the Sabbath from a mere obligation into a cherished, life-giving rhythm that sustains the family's spiritual well-being throughout the entire week.

When we consider the overarching rhythms of faith that can anchor a Christian family, the communal act of worship within the local church stands as a particularly vital practice. While the Sabbath provides a sacred space for rest and family-focused spiritual nourishment, the principle of gathering with fellow believers amplifies our faith journey in unique and essential ways. This participation in corporate worship is not merely a Sunday obligation; it is a dynamic expression of our identity as part of the body of Christ, a cornerstone for fostering a robust and resilient family faith.

It offers a rich tapestry of shared experience, mutual encouragement, and divine instruction that is difficult to replicate in isolation.

The very essence of corporate worship is found in unity and shared purpose. As we gather with other believers, we are reminded that our faith is not an individualistic pursuit, but a communal one. This shared experience of lifting our voices in praise, kneeling in prayer, and listening to the preached Word creates a powerful sense of belonging. For a family, this can be incredibly formative. Children witness firsthand that faith is something that binds people together, transcending individual differences and backgrounds. They see their parents actively participating, engaging with the community, and valuing this sacred time. This modeling is a potent teacher. It communicates that church is not just a place to go, but a community to which we belong, a spiritual family that supports and strengthens us. This sense of belonging is crucial for fostering a lifelong commitment to faith. When children feel connected to their church family, they are more likely to carry that connection into adulthood, finding their own place within the broader Christian community.

Furthermore, the communal aspect of worship provides a vital counterpoint to the often solitary nature of personal devotion. While private prayer and Bible study are indispensable, they can sometimes lead to a narrow perspective. Corporate worship broadens our horizons, exposing us to the diverse gifts and perspectives within the body of Christ. We hear different voices in prayer, encounter various expressions of worship, and are challenged by teachings that may stretch our understanding. This exposure helps to refine our own faith, preventing it from becoming insular or stagnant. For parents, it offers opportunities to discuss theological concepts with their children in a broader context, answering questions and addressing doubts that may arise from hearing different viewpoints. It allows for shared learning and growth that enriches the entire family's spiritual understanding.

The teaching element within corporate worship is another significant benefit. Pastors and teachers are given by God to equip the saints for ministry and to build up the body of Christ. Through sermons, Bible studies, and various ministries within the church, families receive consistent instruction in God's Word. This consistent diet of sound doctrine provides the spiritual nourishment necessary for growth. For children, this teaching often comes in age-appropriate formats through Sunday School, children's church, or youth groups, laying a foundation of biblical knowledge and understanding. The repetition of key biblical truths, presented in different ways by different teachers, helps to cement these truths in young minds. Parents can then build upon this foundation at home, reinforcing the lessons learned and applying them to family life. This synergy between home and church creates a powerful learning environment for children.

Fellowship, a natural outflow of corporate worship, is equally invaluable for family faith. The church is intended to be a place of genuine connection and mutual support. Sharing meals, participating in service projects, or simply engaging in conversations with other families can forge deep bonds. These relationships provide a network of encouragement and accountability, which is particularly beneficial during challenging times. When a family faces difficulties, having other Christian families who can offer prayer, practical help, and wise counsel can make an enormous difference. Conversely, when a family is experiencing blessings, sharing those joys with the church community magnifies the gratitude and fosters a spirit of shared celebration. This interconnectedness strengthens not only individual families but the entire church body. It creates a living testament to the love of Christ, visible to the world.

Making church attendance a priority requires intentionality and a willingness to structure our weekly schedules accordingly. It means recognizing that Sunday is not just another day off, but a day dedicated to God and to His gathered people. This often involves a degree of preparation throughout the week, perhaps by choosing a church that aligns with our family's theological convictions and practical needs, and then committing to regular attendance. It might mean planning meals ahead of time, ensuring laundry is done, and arranging transportation to minimize any last-minute rush or excuse for absence. For families with young children, this preparation can be even more critical, involving packing diaper bags, preparing snacks, and establishing routines that facilitate a smooth transition into the worship service.

Creating a positive and engaging experience of church for the whole family is key to fostering a lasting love for it. This involves more than just showing up; it's about actively participating and fostering a sense of anticipation and enjoyment. For parents, this can mean discussing the upcoming service with children, perhaps previewing a hymn or a Scripture passage that will be featured. It can involve talking about what they learned or enjoyed after the service, encouraging reflection and engagement. For children, it's about helping them understand the significance of what is happening – why we sing, why we listen to the Bible, why we pray. Making church a place of connection, learning, and participation, rather than a passive obligation, can transform it into a cherished weekly event for the entire family.

Consider the impact of involving children in the worship service itself. This might mean giving them a children's bulletin with activities related to the sermon, or encouraging them to listen for certain key words or phrases. For older children, the expectation might be to take notes or to engage in thoughtful reflection on the sermon's application. Even younger children can be involved by having them hold a Bible, point to the words as they are read, or participate in congregational singing. The goal is to foster active engagement rather than passive reception. When children feel like they are a part of the worship, rather than just observers, their experience becomes far more meaningful.

The teaching received at church often serves as a springboard for continued family discussion and discipleship at home. For instance, after a sermon on prayer, parents can set aside time to pray together as a family, perhaps using the principles discussed in the sermon as a guide. If a lesson was taught on forgiveness, families can explore practical ways to practice forgiveness within the home. This integration of church teaching into daily life reinforces spiritual lessons and demonstrates their relevance to real-world situations. It transforms abstract theological concepts into tangible, lived experiences for the family.

Moreover, the church provides a crucial context for understanding our role as disciples in the world. Through various ministries, families can learn to serve others, to share their faith, and to contribute to the work of God in the community. Participating in outreach programs, volunteering for church events, or supporting missions can teach children valuable lessons about generosity, compassion, and the Great Commission. These experiences move faith beyond the four walls of the church building and into the broader community, shaping children into active and engaged followers of Christ. For example, participating in a local food bank drive or a Christmas caroling event at a nursing home can be profoundly impactful experiences for children, demonstrating the practical outworking of their faith.

The commitment to corporate worship also involves a conscious choice to prioritize fellowship with other believers. This can be as simple as inviting another family to join you for lunch after church, or participating in a small group or Bible study. These opportunities for deeper connection allow families to build authentic relationships with those who share their faith. They provide a space for vulnerability, encouragement, and shared growth. When parents model these intentional acts of fellowship, they teach their children the importance of community and the blessings that come from nurturing these relationships. It shows children that faith is lived out in connection with others, not in isolation.

It is also beneficial to discuss with children why attending church is important. Explaining the biblical mandate for gathering, the benefits of corporate worship, and the role of the church in God's plan can help them understand the significance of this practice. Rather than simply stating, "We go to church because we have to," parents can articulate the deeper reasons, fostering a more informed and willing participation. This can involve reading Scripture passages that speak to the importance of gathering, such as Hebrews 10:24-25, and discussing what they mean for your family.

The church also offers a valuable perspective on the diversity of God's creation and the richness of His kingdom. By worshipping alongside people from different backgrounds, cultures, and walks of life, families gain a broader understanding of God's global work. This exposure can cultivate a more inclusive and compassionate worldview in children, teaching them to value and respect all people as children of God. It breaks down ethnocentrism and fosters a global consciousness rooted in the Gospel. Attending a church with a diverse congregation, or participating in international mission trips or partnerships, can be particularly impactful in this regard. Ultimately, the goal is to cultivate a family culture where corporate worship is not seen as a burden, but as a cherished privilege and a vital component of spiritual health. It is about fostering a sense of anticipation for Sunday, of valuing the community of faith, and of actively participating in the life of the church. When parents consistently prioritize and model these aspects of faith, they are laying a strong foundation for their children's enduring walk with God. This consistent engagement strengthens the family's spiritual resilience, deepens their understanding of God's Word, and cultivates a profound sense of belonging within the greater body of Christ. It is in this shared space of worship and fellowship that families can truly grow together in faith, drawing strength from God and from one another as they navigate the journey of life. The act of gathering week after week, united in praise and devotion, becomes a powerful testament to the enduring truth of the Gospel and its transformative power within the family unit. This communal act of faith is a tangible expression of our reliance on God and our commitment to one another as fellow travelers on the path of discipleship.

The journey of faith within a Christian household is profoundly enriched by the intentional practice of weekly scripture study and discussion. Moving beyond passive reception of biblical truths, this deliberate engagement transforms God's Word from an abstract concept into a living, breathing guide for family life. It's in these dedicated times that we, as parents, have a unique opportunity to nurture our children's understanding of God's character, His love for us, and His will for our lives. This isn't about presenting ourselves as all-knowing theologians, but rather as fellow travelers on a path of discovery, eager to explore the riches of Scripture together. The goal is to cultivate a shared spiritual rhythm, one that builds a strong, resilient foundation for faith that can withstand the inevitable challenges of life and celebrate its abundant joys.

When embarking on this journey, the first crucial step is selecting the passages for study. While an overarching yearly plan, perhaps following a lectionary or a specific book of the Bible, can provide structure, there's also immense value in flexibility and responsiveness. Consider topical studies that address current family needs or questions. For instance, if the family is grappling with a particular challenge, like navigating sibling conflict or facing disappointment, a study on forgiveness, perseverance, or trusting God's plan can be incredibly timely and relevant. Alternatively, simply working through a book of the Bible sequentially, chapter by chapter, can provide a comprehensive and systematic understanding of God's redemptive story. The key is to choose passages that are accessible and engaging for all age groups present. Shorter, focused passages are often more effective than trying to tackle lengthy, complex chapters, especially when children are young. Think about the age range of your children and select verses that can be easily grasped and discussed. For very young children, a single verse or a short story from the Gospels might be ideal, while older children and teenagers can engage with more complex theological concepts and longer narratives. Don't be afraid to revisit passages, as repeated exposure often deepens understanding and reveals new layers of meaning. The Holy Spirit is our ultimate teacher, and He can illuminate even the most familiar verses in fresh and powerful ways.

Facilitating these discussions requires creating a safe and inviting atmosphere where every voice is valued. This means actively listening, asking open-ended questions, and encouraging participation from every family member, regardless of age. For the youngest members, questions can be simple and concrete: "What did Jesus do in this story?" "How did the people feel?" "What did God ask them to do?" For older children and teenagers, questions can delve deeper into application and interpretation: "What does this passage teach us about God's character?" "How does this apply to our lives today?" "Are there any parts of this passage that are confusing or challenging?" It's important to create an environment where it's okay not to know the answer, and where exploring different perspectives is encouraged. Avoid the temptation to simply lecture or provide all the answers yourself. Instead, foster a spirit of inquiry and shared discovery. Sometimes, simply asking "What stands out to you in this passage?" can open up unexpected avenues of discussion. Encourage children to share their personal connections to the text, even if those connections seem simple or tangential. These are often the entry points for deeper spiritual growth. Remember, the goal is not to have a perfect theological debate, but to foster a love for God's Word and a desire to understand it more deeply.

Applying biblical truths to daily life is where scripture study truly comes alive. The Bible is not meant to be a purely academic pursuit; it is a practical guide for living. After studying a passage, dedicate time to discussing how its principles can be lived out in tangible ways. If you've studied a passage on kindness, brainstorm specific ways your family can show kindness to neighbors, friends, or even strangers. If you've explored a passage on honesty, discuss situations where honesty is crucial and how to uphold it. This practical application bridges the gap between Sunday theology and weekday reality. It transforms abstract commands into actionable steps, making faith a living reality within the home. For example, after studying the parable of the Good Samaritan, your family could plan to volunteer at a local shelter or identify someone in your community who might need assistance and intentionally reach out. This makes the biblical narrative relevant and imprints its values onto the hearts of your children. It also provides invaluable teachable moments when unexpected situations arise. When a child is faced with a temptation to lie or a conflict with a sibling, you can gently guide them back to the principles you've studied together, offering a biblical framework for their decisions. This consistent reinforcement strengthens their understanding and builds a strong moral compass guided by God's Word.

The regularity of this practice is paramount. Establishing a consistent time and place for scripture study, even if it's just 15-20 minutes a few times a week, signals its importance to your family. It becomes a predictable and cherished rhythm in the week, a time to intentionally connect with God and with each other. This consistency also builds spiritual discipline, not just for the children, but for the parents as well. It requires commitment and a willingness to prioritize spiritual nourishment. Consider designating a specific evening or a quiet morning hour for this practice. Make it a special time, perhaps by lighting a candle, having a special snack, or using a family Bible that has been passed down through generations. The sacredness of the time, even in its simplicity, can enhance its impact. It's about creating a spiritual anchor in the midst of busy schedules and competing demands.

Furthermore, incorporate a variety of methods to keep scripture study engaging and dynamic. While reading directly from the Bible is essential, consider supplementing your study with other resources. Age-appropriate story Bibles can be excellent for younger children, retelling biblical narratives in ways that are captivating and understandable. Visual aids, such as maps, timelines, or even simple drawings created by the children as they listen, can enhance comprehension. For older children, engaging with commentaries designed for teens or young adults, or exploring interactive Bible study apps, can add another dimension to their learning. Some families find it beneficial to memorize scripture together, choosing verses that are particularly meaningful or relevant to their family's journey. This memorization not only instills God's Word in their hearts but also provides them with powerful tools for spiritual warfare and encouragement in difficult times. The act of memorization itself is a form of deep engagement with the text, requiring focused attention and repetition.

The beauty of this weekly practice lies in its cumulative effect. Each session, however brief, adds to a growing reservoir of biblical knowledge and spiritual understanding. Over time, children will begin to internalize the truths of God's Word, not just intellectually, but experientially. They will develop a framework for understanding the world through a biblical lens, enabling them to discern truth from error and to make wise choices. This consistent immersion in Scripture is the foundation for a lifelong, vibrant faith. It equips them to navigate the complexities of life with wisdom, courage, and unwavering hope in Christ. It also strengthens the family unit, creating a shared spiritual identity and a common language of faith. As you read, discuss, and apply God's Word together, you are building a legacy of faith that will extend far beyond your own generation.

This intentionality in scripture study is a testament to our faith and our love for our children. It is an investment in their eternal well-being, a sowing of seeds that, by God's grace, will yield a bountiful harvest. It's in these moments of shared exploration of God's Word that the family truly becomes a discipleship unit, learning together, growing together, and being transformed together by the power of the Gospel. The Holy Spirit, who inspired the Scriptures, is present to illuminate their meaning and to apply their truth to our hearts and lives. By prioritizing this practice, we are actively participating in God's work of sanctification within our own families, laying a foundation that will support and strengthen them through every season of life. It is a sacred trust and a profound joy to guide our children in understanding and loving the very words of God.

The selection of scripture passages can be approached with both structure and spontaneity. One effective method is to cycle through different genres of biblical literature. Perhaps one week you focus on a Psalm that speaks of God's comfort, the next on a parable from the Gospels that illustrates a key spiritual principle, and the following week on a narrative from the Old Testament that reveals God's faithfulness. This variety keeps the study fresh and exposes the family to the breadth and depth of God's revelation. Another approach is to tie the scripture study to the church's sermon or Sunday School lessons. This reinforces what children are hearing at a more formal level of teaching and provides an opportunity to dig deeper into the themes presented. For example, if the sermon was about the Fruit of the Spirit, your family could spend time studying Galatians 5:22-23 verse by verse, discussing what each fruit looks like in practice. This can be a particularly effective way to bridge the gap between corporate worship and home discipleship, ensuring that the biblical content is relevant and integrated into family life.

When facilitating discussions, remember that active listening is as important as speaking. Allow for pauses, and don't be afraid of silence. Often, a moment of quiet contemplation can lead to deeper reflection and more meaningful contributions. Encourage children to ask clarifying questions, and if you don't know the answer, model a healthy response: "That's a great question! Let's look that up together," or "I'm not sure about that, but we can pray about it and seek God's wisdom." This demonstrates humility and a commitment to seeking truth, rather than always having to be the expert. For younger children, using visual aids such as flannelgraph stories, puppets, or even simple drawings can make biblical narratives come alive. They can also be encouraged to act out the stories after hearing them. For older children, journaling their thoughts and questions about the passage can be a valuable tool, allowing them to process the information independently and then share their insights.

The application of biblical truths can be made concrete through a variety of family activities. If you've studied a passage on stewardship, your family could together plan a budget for a portion of your income to be given to a ministry or a family in need. If you've learned about perseverance from the story of Joseph, you could discuss a challenge each family member is facing and brainstorm ways to persevere through it, perhaps by encouraging each other with Scripture. Creating a "Bible Truth Challenge" for the week can also be fun and engaging. For instance, after studying a passage on gratitude, challenge everyone to find three new things to be thankful for each day and share them at dinner. This habit of actively seeking out God's blessings can transform a family's perspective and cultivate a more joyful outlook on life.

The frequency and duration of scripture study sessions are flexible and should be adapted to your family's unique needs and circumstances. While a daily practice is ideal for those who can manage it, a consistent weekly rhythm is a strong and achievable goal. Even a short, focused session of 20-30 minutes can be highly impactful. The key is consistency and intentionality. It's better to have a shorter, regular time of study than sporadic, lengthy sessions. Consider integrating scripture study into existing family routines. Perhaps it's during a weekend breakfast, a quiet evening after dinner, or even a car ride if you're traveling together. The more seamlessly it fits into the natural flow of family life, the more likely it is to become an established and cherished habit.

As children grow, their capacity for understanding and engaging with Scripture will also evolve. For preschoolers, simple Bible stories with clear moral lessons and repetitive elements are most effective. They can also participate in singing praise songs that are rich in biblical truth. Elementary-aged children can engage with more detailed narratives, begin to understand basic theological concepts, and participate in age-appropriate discussions. They may also enjoy activities like creating Bible crafts or memorizing shorter verses. Teenagers can handle more complex theological discussions, wrestle with difficult biblical passages, and apply principles to their own emerging worldview. It's important to tailor the approach to each developmental stage, ensuring that the content and methods remain engaging and relevant.

The impact of consistent, shared scripture study extends far beyond the immediate. It cultivates a spiritual vocabulary, a shared understanding of God's character and His plan for humanity, and a common ground for family discussions about life's most important issues. It provides children with a biblical framework for understanding themselves, others, and the world around them, equipping them to make wise decisions and to live lives that honor God. This practice is a powerful tool for spiritual formation, building a strong foundation of faith that will serve them throughout their lives. It is an act of love, obedience, and a testament to the enduring power of God's Word to transform hearts and homes.

The journey of spiritual growth within a Christian family is not solely confined to the pages of Scripture or the quiet moments of prayer; it blossoms vibrantly when extended outwards through acts of service and compassion. In the previous section, we explored the foundational importance of delving into God's Word together. Now, we pivot to the vital practice of embodying those truths in the world around us, demonstrating God's love not just in word, but in tangible deed. This is where the sacredness of our faith truly intersects with the needs of our community, transforming our families into living testaments to the Gospel. Cultivating a heart for service in our children, and indeed in ourselves, is a profound aspect of discipleship, mirroring the selfless love that Christ so powerfully displayed. It's about intentionally weaving opportunities to serve into the fabric of our weekly rhythm, fostering a spirit of generosity and empathy that reflects the very character of our Heavenly Father.

Our faith calls us to be the hands and feet of Jesus in a world that so often feels broken and in need of His healing touch. This means looking beyond the comfortable confines of our homes and our immediate circle of loved ones to identify those who are struggling, overlooked, or in need of a helping hand. It's about actively seeking out avenues to share God's abundant love, not as an obligation, but as a joyful overflow of a heart transformed by His grace. The beauty of integrating acts of service into our family life is that it serves a dual purpose: it blesses those we serve, and it profoundly blesses us in return, shaping our perspectives and deepening our gratitude for all that we have.

One of the most accessible and impactful ways to begin is by identifying needs within our local church community. Our churches are vibrant bodies of believers, and within them, there are often individuals or families facing particular challenges – perhaps a new mother overwhelmed with newborn care, an elderly parishioner struggling with mobility, or a family going through a financial hardship. These are often opportunities for simple, yet meaningful, acts of service. A meal train, where families take turns preparing and delivering a nourishing meal, can be a tremendous blessing. It's not just about the food itself, but the tangible message of "we see you, we care about you, and you are not alone." This can be organized through a church committee or simply initiated by a few families who feel called to serve. For younger children, participating in this can involve helping to pack the meal, decorate a container, or even drawing a picture to include with the delivery.

Beyond the church walls, our neighborhoods present countless opportunities. Think about the elderly couple down the street who may have difficulty with yard work, the single parent juggling multiple responsibilities who could benefit from a few hours of childcare, or the family that has recently moved in and might appreciate a welcome basket with some essentials and a friendly face. Even simple gestures, like baking cookies for a neighbor or offering to pick up their mail while they're away, can build bridges and demonstrate Christ's love. These acts, while seemingly small, can have a ripple effect, creating a more connected and caring community. When children are involved in these initiatives, they learn firsthand about the value of neighborly love and the importance of looking out for one another. They see that service isn't just for grand occasions, but for the everyday moments that make up life.

For families with older children and teenagers, more structured volunteer opportunities can be incredibly enriching. Many local organizations are always in need of volunteers, and choosing a cause that resonates with your family's values can be a powerful way to serve. This could involve dedicating a Saturday morning to serving meals at a homeless shelter, spending an afternoon at an animal rescue, or participating in a community clean-up event. The key is to involve the children in the selection process, allowing them to have a voice in where and how their time is invested. This fosters a sense of ownership and commitment to the cause. Discussions during and after these experiences are crucial. What did they observe? How did it make them feel? What did they learn about the people or issues they encountered? These conversations help solidify the lessons of empathy and social responsibility.

Another profound way to cultivate a spirit of compassion is through direct engagement with those who are marginalized or less fortunate. This might include visiting nursing homes, where residents often crave companionship and conversation. Even a simple visit from a family, with children sharing artwork or singing songs, can brighten someone's day immeasurably. Similarly, supporting local food banks or homeless shelters, whether through donating goods or volunteering time to sort donations, teaches children about the reality of poverty and the importance of generosity. It's about opening their eyes to the diverse needs within society and instilling in them a desire to make a positive difference.

The act of giving is also a powerful aspect of service. This can extend beyond monetary donations to giving of our time, our talents, and even our possessions. Perhaps your family has outgrown clothing or toys that could be donated to a local charity. Teaching children to declutter and share what they have is a valuable lesson in contentment and generosity. It helps them understand that possessions are not meant to be hoarded but can be a means of blessing others. When children are involved in the process of selecting items to donate, they gain a tangible understanding of sharing and sacrifice.

Furthermore, incorporating acts of service can also be a way to respond to specific biblical themes or events. For instance, during the Advent season, families might choose to "adopt" a family in need, purchasing gifts and food for them. Or after studying a parable like the Good Samaritan, the family could intentionally seek out someone in their community who needs help and offer assistance. This direct application of biblical principles makes faith practical and memorable. It bridges the gap between hearing about God's love and actively participating in its demonstration.

The benefits of engaging in these acts of service are multifaceted and deeply impactful on the spiritual formation of our families. Firstly, it cultivates humility. When we serve those who may have less than us, or who face greater challenges, it provides a powerful antidote to entitlement and pride. It reminds us of God's abundant grace and fosters a deep sense of gratitude for our own blessings. Children, in particular, are naturally egocentric to some extent, and regular exposure to serving others helps shift their focus outwards, fostering empathy and a more Christ-like perspective. They begin to understand that their own comfort and well-being are not the ultimate measure of success.

Secondly, these experiences build compassion. By encountering different life circumstances and hearing the stories of others, children develop a greater capacity for empathy. They learn to put themselves in others' shoes, to understand their struggles, and to feel a genuine desire to alleviate their suffering. This emotional intelligence is a crucial component of spiritual maturity, enabling them to connect with others on a deeper level and to respond with love and understanding. It transforms abstract notions of "loving your neighbor" into lived experience.

Thirdly, acts of service foster a sense of purpose and fulfillment. Knowing that they have made a positive difference in someone else's life, however small, can be incredibly empowering for children and adults alike. It instills a sense of agency and demonstrates that even ordinary people, empowered by God, can bring about meaningful change. This can also combat feelings of helplessness or apathy that can sometimes arise when faced with the world's vast problems. By engaging in tangible acts of service, we are actively participating in God's redemptive work, and that is a deeply rewarding experience.

Moreover, these shared experiences strengthen family bonds. Working together towards a common goal, serving alongside each other, and discussing the impact of your efforts creates shared memories and a common purpose. It provides opportunities for parents to model faith in action, to teach valuable life lessons, and to have meaningful conversations about values, priorities, and the nature of God's love. These are the moments that often become cherished family traditions and contribute to a strong, shared spiritual identity. The teamwork involved in, for example, organizing a food drive or cleaning up a local park, reinforces cooperation and shared responsibility.

It's also important to remember that service isn't always about grand gestures or organized events. Many of the most impactful acts of service are the quiet, consistent, everyday actions that demonstrate love and care. This could be offering a listening ear to a friend who is struggling, praying for someone by name, or simply speaking words of encouragement to a family member. Teaching children to recognize and respond to these everyday opportunities for service is just as vital as participating in larger initiatives. It cultivates a mindset of service that is woven into the very fabric of their being, rather than being an occasional activity.

When we integrate acts of service and compassion into our family's weekly rhythm, we are not merely adding another item to our schedule. We are actively cultivating a spiritual discipline that shapes hearts, builds character, and allows God's love to flow through our homes and into the world. It is a tangible expression of our faith, a powerful way to teach our children about the self-giving love of Christ, and a beautiful testament to the transformative power of a family committed to serving Him. The process of identifying needs, planning how to meet them, and then carrying out those plans together provides invaluable lessons in stewardship, responsibility, and empathy. It is through these shared experiences of active love that our families truly become discipleship units, learning to live out the Gospel in practical, impactful ways. This commitment to service is a continuous journey, one that evolves with the age and abilities of our children, always pointing us back to the heart of God and His boundless love for humanity. The legacy we build is not just in what we teach, but in how we live, demonstrating that faith is most potent when it is put into practice.

The spiritual journey of a family is not a static destination but a dynamic, unfolding process. As we transition from the grounding practices of Scripture and outward acts of service, it becomes clear that intentionality is the bedrock upon which sustained spiritual growth is built. This intentionality requires us to pause, to reflect, and to look forward with purpose. Therefore, dedicating a specific time each week for family reflection and planning is not merely an organizational tool; it is a vital spiritual discipline that anchors our shared faith journey, ensuring that our spiritual aspirations remain vibrant and actively pursued amidst the ebb and flow of daily life. Imagine the close of a Sunday, a day set apart for worship and spiritual nourishment. As the week draws to a close, and the anticipation of the coming days begins to stir, this is an opportune moment for a dedicated family gathering. It needn't be a lengthy or formal affair, but rather a time carved out with intention, perhaps over a simple dessert, during a leisurely walk, or simply gathered around the kitchen table. This is our opportunity to pause, breathe, and connect as a family on a spiritual level, reviewing the past week's journey with God and preparing our hearts and minds for the days that lie ahead. This ritual reinforces our shared commitment to Christ, fostering unity and mutual encouragement as we navigate life together.

The essence of this family reflection lies in looking back with gratitude and discernment. What were the moments this past week when God's presence felt particularly strong? Where did we see His hand at work in our lives, whether in moments of joy, in answered prayers, or in unexpected blessings? These are the triumphs we want to celebrate, the evidence of God's faithfulness that strengthens our faith and reminds us of His constant presence. It is also important to acknowledge where we may have stumbled or faced challenges. Were there moments of frustration, doubt, or perhaps times when we failed to live out our faith as we intended? These are not occasions for condemnation, but for honest self-assessment, repentance, and seeking God's forgiveness and strength. Openly discussing these aspects within the family creates a safe space for vulnerability and mutual support. For instance, a child might share their struggle with a particular temptation they faced at school, or a parent might admit to feeling overwhelmed by a situation at work. This shared honesty builds trust and allows for guided prayer and encouragement.

When we engage in this reflection, we are not merely recounting events; we are seeking to understand God's work within and through our family. We can ask questions like, "Where did we see love demonstrated this week, either by us or towards us?" or "Were there opportunities to share our faith or to show God's kindness that we missed or embraced?" This process helps us to discern the spiritual currents in our lives, to identify patterns, and to learn from our experiences. It's about moving beyond simply going through the motions of faith and actively engaging with God's Word and His Spirit in the practicalities of our daily existence. This intentional review can also involve discussing how our family's spiritual goals are progressing. Did we manage to read the Bible together as planned? Were our family prayer times consistent? Did we actively seek opportunities to serve others? This honest assessment helps us to adjust our approach and to recommit to our shared vision.

Following this period of reflection, the focus shifts to planning for the week ahead. This is where we move from looking back to looking forward with intentionality. What are our family's spiritual priorities for the coming days? How can we ensure that our faith remains central, not just in our private devotion, but in our shared family life? This might involve deciding which Bible passages to focus on, scheduling a family prayer time, or planning a specific act of service. For example, if the family is studying a particular biblical character, the plan for the week might include looking for ways to emulate that character's faith or courage in their own lives. If the previous week

166

revealed a struggle with gossip, the plan for the upcoming week could involve a conscious effort to speak words of encouragement and edification to one another and to those outside the home.

The planning process is also an opportunity to intercede for one another and for the week's challenges. Each family member can share specific needs or concerns they have for the upcoming days. This might include upcoming exams, difficult conversations, health concerns, or the need for patience in a trying situation. As a family, we can then lift these intentions to God in prayer, creating a powerful shield of faith around our week. This shared prayer time reinforces the understanding that we are not alone in our struggles, but that we have a Heavenly Father who cares for every detail of our lives and a family united in prayer to support one another. It's a tangible way to bring our hopes and fears before God, trusting in His providence and His ability to guide us.

Consider the practicalities of this weekly planning. It might involve looking at the family calendar together and identifying potential spiritual opportunities or challenges. For instance, a busy week with multiple activities might require scheduling a shorter, more focused prayer session rather than a longer one. Or, if a family member is facing a significant event, the plan could include specific prayers and encouragement leading up to it. This isn't about imposing rigid structure, but about mindful stewardship of our time and energy, ensuring that our spiritual life is not an afterthought, but a foundational element woven into the fabric of our week. The goal is to be proactive rather than reactive, to set our intentions before the week's demands begin to dictate our direction.

This intentional family gathering also serves to strengthen our family unit. When we share our reflections, our triumphs, and our struggles, we build deeper intimacy and understanding. We learn to celebrate each other's spiritual victories and to offer comfort and support during times of difficulty. This shared vulnerability and mutual encouragement create a stronger, more cohesive family unit, bound together by a common faith and a shared journey. It's in these moments of open communication and prayer that the spiritual discipleship of children is most profoundly nurtured, as they witness their parents actively engaging with God and with each other in faith. They see that faith is not just learned, but lived.

Moreover, this practice cultivates a spirit of unity and shared purpose within the family. By actively involving each member in the reflection and planning process, everyone feels a sense of ownership and responsibility for the family's spiritual growth. Children, when given the opportunity to contribute their thoughts and prayers, develop a deeper connection to the family's spiritual life. They understand that their faith journey is integral to the family's collective journey. This shared ownership fosters a stronger sense of belonging and a united front as we face the world together, rooted in our faith.

The transition to planning for the week ahead is where our faith becomes actionable. We might pray for wisdom for upcoming decisions, for opportunities to share the Gospel, or for the strength to overcome specific temptations. This proactive approach to spiritual living ensures that our faith is not confined to Sunday mornings but permeates every aspect of our lives. It's about asking, "How can we, as a family, be more like Christ this week?" and then making concrete plans to do so. This could involve a commitment to showing patience, extending grace, or actively seeking out those in need. For example, if a family member has been struggling with anger, the plan might include specific strategies for managing frustration and a family prayer for increased self-control and gentleness.

This weekly ritual also helps us to keep our spiritual goals in focus. In the midst of busy schedules and competing demands, it's easy for our spiritual aspirations to get sidelined. By dedicating this time to reflection and planning, we intentionally bring our spiritual priorities back to the forefront. We are reminded of what truly matters, and we are equipped to make choices that align with our faith. This consistent reinforcement ensures that our family's spiritual journey is not haphazard but guided by purpose and intentionality. It's about being mindful stewards of the spiritual gifts and responsibilities God has entrusted to us as a family.

The beauty of this family reflection and planning lies in its adaptability. It can be tailored to the age and developmental stage of the children. For younger children, the focus might be on simple expressions of gratitude, identifying moments of kindness, and praying basic prayers. As children mature, they can be encouraged to take on more active roles in sharing their reflections, identifying needs, and contributing to the prayer requests. The goal is always to foster an environment where faith is discussed openly, celebrated, and actively lived out within the family context. The process itself becomes a teaching moment, demonstrating that faith is a living, breathing aspect of our family identity.

Ultimately, this dedicated time for family reflection and planning is a powerful tool for fostering a deeply rooted, vibrant spiritual life within our homes. It encourages intentionality, builds unity, strengthens family bonds, and equips us to face the week ahead with faith and purpose. It's a testament to our commitment as a family to walk with Christ, learning, growing, and serving together, day by day. By pausing to reflect and plan, we are not just managing our schedules; we are actively participating in God's ongoing work in our lives, ensuring that our family remains a beacon of His love and truth in the world. This weekly habit transforms our faith from a passive belief into an active, shared pursuit, creating a legacy of spiritual commitment that will undoubtedly shape generations to come. It reinforces that our family's spiritual health is a priority, worth intentional effort and focused time.

Chapter 7: Monthly Spiritual Refreshment and Growth

Beyond the weekly rhythm of reflection and planning, there are seasons within the spiritual journey that call for a deeper, more concentrated immersion in God's presence. This is where the powerful disciplines of dedicated prayer and fasting periods come into play, offering a unique pathway to spiritual refreshment and accelerated growth for our families. Just as our bodies benefit from periods of rest and intentional nourishment, so too does our spiritual life thrive when we set aside regular times for concentrated prayer and, when biblically appropriate, fasting. These are not mere rituals to be performed, but vibrant expressions of our dependence on the Almighty, opportunities to draw closer to Him, and avenues through which He can refine and strengthen us as individuals and as a family unit.

The biblical precedent for dedicated periods of prayer and fasting is rich and instructive. From Moses on Mount Sinai to David in times of crisis, from Esther rallying her people to Jesus Himself in the wilderness, Scripture reveals individuals and communities turning to fasting and prayer as vital tools for seeking divine intervention, confirmation, and strength. These accounts are not relics of a bygone era; they are living testimonies to the enduring power of these disciplines in the life of faith. When we engage in them, we are participating in a lineage of believers who have discovered firsthand that drawing near to God in this focused manner can yield profound spiritual transformation. It's about moving beyond the everyday cadence of prayer to a deliberate, intentional outpouring of our hearts before the Father, often accompanied by a conscious abstaining from something that sustains us physically, thereby elevating our spiritual focus.

The essence of fasting, when embraced within a family context, is not about self-punishment or earning God's favor. Rather, it is a spiritual discipline designed to heighten our awareness of God's presence and our need for Him. By voluntarily abstaining from food, or another

171

common comfort, for a set period, we are essentially saying, "Lord, You are more important than this." This act redirects our focus from physical sustenance to spiritual nourishment. It can break the hold of our appetites and desires, opening our hearts and minds to receive what God has for us. For families, this can be a particularly potent way to cultivate a shared sense of seeking, to unite in a common spiritual pursuit that transcends individual preferences and strengthens the bonds of faith within the home. It's a tangible way to say, "We are in this together, seeking You."

When considering family fasting, it is crucial to approach it with wisdom, love, and consideration for the age and health of each family member. Not all forms of fasting are suitable for every individual. For families with young children, a full day of fasting from food might not be appropriate. Instead, consider partial fasts, such as abstaining from a particular meal, or even a fast from specific activities that consume our time and attention, like screen time or social media, for a designated period. The principle remains the same: to intentionally create space in our lives to focus more intently on God. For instance, a family might decide to fast from desserts for a week, dedicating the saved time and the mental energy usually spent anticipating that treat to prayer and Bible study. Or perhaps, a weekend fast from all electronic devices, channeling that time into shared activities, conversations, and focused prayer. The key is the intentionality behind the sacrifice and the redirection of energy toward spiritual pursuits.

Setting aside dedicated periods for prayer and fasting within the family allows us to approach God with specific intentions, seeking His guidance on significant decisions, praying for breakthroughs in challenging circumstances, or simply desiring a deeper intimacy with Him. These extended prayer times can be structured or free-flowing, depending on what best suits your family. It might involve gathering at specific times throughout the day—perhaps upon waking, before meals, and before bed—to pray corporately. Creating a prayer journal where family members can write down their requests and thank-yous can also be a powerful tool, allowing everyone to see how God has answered prayers and to maintain focus on what is being sought. This shared experience of petition and praise fosters a sense of unity and purpose, reminding us that we are a spiritual unit navigating life together under God's care.

The spiritual sensitivity that fasting can cultivate is a remarkable benefit. When our physical appetites are subdued, our spiritual senses often become more acute. We may find ourselves more attuned to the promptings of the Holy Spirit, more receptive to God's voice, and more keenly aware of the spiritual battles we face. This heightened sensitivity can be particularly beneficial for families navigating difficult seasons, such as dealing with illness, relational conflict, or significant life transitions. A concentrated period of prayer and fasting can serve as a spiritual reset, clearing away the distractions and noise of daily life to hear God's direction with greater clarity and to find His strength to persevere.

Moreover, engaging in these disciplines together teaches our children invaluable lessons about faith and reliance on God. They learn that prayer is not just a casual request, but a powerful tool that can move mountains. They witness firsthand the benefits of fasting as a means of drawing closer to God and seeking His will. This shared practice instills in them a practical understanding of spiritual warfare and the importance of spiritual disciplines in their own lives. It's a hands-on education in the power of a surrendered heart and a united voice raised in prayer. For example, if the family is facing a particular challenge, such as a difficult job situation for a parent or a relational struggle for a child, dedicating a period to prayer and fasting can empower the family to face it together, with a shared sense of hope and trust in God's provision.

When we commit to these focused times of prayer and fasting, we are actively choosing to prioritize our spiritual walk, both individually and as a family. It's an intentional act of stepping away from the ordinary to embrace the extraordinary work of God in our lives. This can involve setting aside a full day, a weekend, or even a specific week each month or quarter for this deeper engagement. The duration and intensity can be adapted to your family's capacity and current circumstances, but the commitment to the principle of concentrated spiritual pursuit remains the core. It's about carving out sacred time, unburdened by the usual demands, to commune with the Creator, to seek His face, and to allow His Spirit to refresh and renew us.

Consider the impact of a family fast during a significant time, such as before making a major family decision, like a move or a significant financial investment, or during a season of national or global concern. In such moments, a unified approach to seeking God's wisdom and direction can bring immense peace and clarity. Each family member can be encouraged to identify specific prayer points related to the situation, and the fasting period becomes a tangible expression of their collective earnestness. This shared experience can forge an even stronger bond within the family, as they witness God's faithfulness in responding to their united prayers. It's a testament to the power of "two or three" gathered together in His name, amplified by the intentional act of fasting.

Furthermore, these dedicated periods can serve as a powerful antidote to spiritual complacency. In the busyness of life, it's easy to fall into a routine where our faith feels more like an obligation than a vibrant relationship. Fasting and extended prayer time disrupt this complacency, jolting us back into a posture of dependence and hunger for God. It reminds us that our strength comes from Him alone and that He desires a deep, intimate connection with us. This intentional recalibration is essential for maintaining spiritual vitality and ensuring that our faith remains a dynamic force in our lives, rather than a static belief system. It's about actively pursuing God, rather than passively waiting for Him to act.

When planning these dedicated periods, consider creating a sacred space within your home. This might be a corner of the living room, a specific chair, or even just a designated time where distractions are minimized, and the focus is solely on God. Reading aloud Scripture passages that speak to prayer, fasting, and God's power can set the tone. Sharing testimonies of how God has answered prayers in the past, either within your family or from biblical accounts, can also inspire faith and encourage participation. The goal is to create an atmosphere that is conducive to encountering God, an atmosphere of reverence and expectation.

It is also beneficial to discuss the biblical rationale for fasting within the family. Explaining that fasting is not about appeasing God, but about aligning our hearts with His and amplifying our prayers, can help family members understand its purpose. Jesus Himself addressed fasting in Matthew 6:16-18, emphasizing that it should be done with a joyful heart and not for outward recognition. This understanding helps to frame fasting as a positive and empowering spiritual practice, rather than a burdensome or secretive one. By teaching these foundational truths, we equip our children to embrace fasting not as a chore, but as a privilege and a powerful avenue for spiritual connection.

In practice, this might look like a family choosing to fast from dinner one evening a week, dedicating that hour to praying through a specific list of family concerns or praying for others. Or perhaps, a monthly "Day of Prayer and Fasting" where the family commits to shorter, focused prayer sessions throughout the day, abstaining from a particular food or beverage. The key is consistency and intentionality. Even small, consistent steps in dedicated prayer and fasting can yield significant spiritual dividends over time, deepening your family's reliance on God and His provision. It's about building a spiritual muscle that grows stronger with each use, preparing your family to face life's challenges with faith and resilience. This intentional practice serves as a consistent reminder that we are never truly alone, that a loving and powerful God is always present, ready to hear and to answer the earnest prayers of His people, especially when they come from hearts united in faith and willing to sacrifice for deeper communion.

As we move beyond the immediate impact of dedicated prayer and fasting, the journey of spiritual refreshment and growth for our families can be further deepened through focused study and theological exploration. The rhythm of our spiritual lives is not solely about moments of intense seeking, but also about the steady, consistent building of a strong biblical foundation. This involves setting aside specific periods, perhaps a particular month each quarter, or even a concentrated week, to immerse ourselves in a deeper understanding of God's Word and the rich tapestry of Christian theology. This intentional engagement with more complex spiritual concepts can profoundly broaden our perspectives, sharpen our intellect in matters of faith, and foster a more robust, well-reasoned understanding of who God is and what He has done. It's about moving from a foundational knowledge to a more nuanced appreciation of the divine truths that shape our lives.

This proactive approach to theological exploration is not meant to be an academic exercise detached from daily life, but rather a means to infuse our everyday experiences with a deeper, more informed faith. Imagine dedicating a month to understanding the attributes of God, delving into passages that reveal His sovereignty, His love, His justice, and His mercy. This could involve reading a reputable book on the subject, perhaps one that breaks down complex theological concepts into relatable terms, and then discussing specific passages as a family. For instance, when exploring God's sovereignty, you might read about His foreknowledge and His ultimate control over all things, discussing how this truth can bring comfort and peace during times of uncertainty. Conversely, exploring God's justice can lead to conversations about fairness, accountability, and the importance of living righteously in our own lives. This kind of study equips us to understand God not just as a loving Father, but also as a righteous and all-powerful Creator, fostering a more complete and awe-inspiring view of Him.

Another avenue for this deeper study could be to choose a specific book of the Bible and work through it together, chapter by chapter. While any book of Scripture offers immense spiritual value, some lend themselves particularly well to extended family study. Consider the Gospels, for example, where the life, teachings, death, and resurrection of Jesus are presented. Dedicating a month to meticulously studying the Gospel of John, for instance, can offer profound insights into the identity of Christ, His relationship with the Father, and the nature of eternal life. This might involve assigning specific chapters to different family members to read aloud or to prepare a brief summary of. Engaging with commentaries or devotional guides that are specifically geared towards family or group study can also be invaluable. These resources often provide historical context, explain difficult passages, and offer discussion questions that stimulate thoughtful interaction and personal reflection. The goal is not to become instant theologians, but to cultivate a habit of diligent, inquisitive study that builds confidence in our understanding of God's Word.

Theological exploration also provides a framework for understanding the overarching narrative of Scripture. Instead of viewing the Bible as a collection of disconnected stories and commands, a deeper study can reveal the unfolding story of God's redemption plan throughout history. This could involve exploring a theme like covenant, tracing how God established covenants with Abraham, Moses, and David, ultimately culminating in the New Covenant established through Jesus Christ. Understanding these foundational theological concepts helps us to see the continuity and consistency of God's character and His purposes. It can also answer many of the "why" questions that naturally arise as we encounter different passages and teachings. For example, understanding the concept of sin and its consequences helps us to grasp the profound significance of Christ's sacrifice and the grace that is offered to us.

When introducing more complex theological ideas to children, the key is to tailor the approach to their age and comprehension level. For younger children, abstract theological concepts might be best illustrated through stories, analogies, and practical application. For instance, when discussing the doctrine of the Trinity, instead of getting lost in complex philosophical explanations, you might use the analogy of water, which can exist as ice, liquid, and steam, yet remains H2O. Or, you could discuss the idea of a family, where there is a father, mother, and child, each distinct but united in love and purpose. For older children and teenagers, more in-depth discussions, the use of theological dictionaries or encyclopedias, and even engaging with apologetics resources can be highly beneficial. These resources can help them understand the intellectual underpinnings of their faith and equip them to articulate their beliefs in a world that often questions or dismisses them.

Furthermore, setting aside a specific month for theological exploration can provide a structured way to address doctrinal questions or areas of confusion that may arise within the family. Perhaps a sermon or a news event has sparked a question about a particular aspect of Christian belief. Rather than letting the question linger or seeking potentially unreliable answers online, this dedicated time can be used to collectively investigate the topic from a biblical perspective. This demonstrates to children that seeking truth is an ongoing, important process and that the family can be a safe space for exploring difficult questions. It fosters an environment of intellectual honesty and spiritual maturity.

The choice of resources for this deeper study is crucial. Beyond the Bible itself, a curated selection of Christian literature can be immensely helpful. Consider investing in a good study Bible with extensive notes and cross-references. Theological dictionaries and encyclopedias can provide concise explanations of key terms and concepts. For families, devotional books that delve into specific theological themes or books of the Bible can be particularly effective, as they often blend doctrinal teaching with practical application and reflection questions. Websites and podcasts from reputable Christian ministries and scholars can also be excellent supplementary resources, offering accessible explanations of complex ideas. It's important to vet these resources carefully, ensuring they align with sound biblical teaching.

The impact of this intentional theological study extends beyond intellectual understanding; it can profoundly shape a family's worldview and their engagement with the world around them. When we understand biblical principles related to justice, compassion, stewardship, and truth, we are better equipped to navigate the complexities of modern life and to make decisions that honor God. For example, a family that has studied biblical principles of stewardship might engage in more intentional conversations about budgeting, generosity, and responsible use of resources. Likewise, a deep dive into the biblical call to love our neighbor can inspire practical acts of service and a more compassionate approach to social issues. This is where faith moves from being a private matter to a transformative force that impacts every aspect of our lives.

Consider the benefit of collectively studying the book of Romans. This epistle, rich with theological depth, systematically lays out the gospel message, addressing concepts like sin, justification, sanctification, and the sovereignty of God. Working through Romans as a family can provide a solid framework for understanding the core tenets of Christian faith. Discussions could revolve around what it truly means to be justified by faith, the process of becoming more like Christ, and the assurance of salvation. These are not merely academic discussions; they are conversations that can bring immense comfort, assurance, and a deeper understanding of the transformative power of God's grace in our lives.

Moreover, engaging in this type of in-depth study cultivates a shared language and understanding within the family concerning spiritual matters. When specific theological terms or concepts become familiar through repeated study and discussion, it facilitates more effective communication about faith. It can lead to more meaningful conversations during prayer times, in times of crisis, or when discussing life decisions. This shared spiritual vocabulary builds a stronger sense of unity and purpose, as family members are on the same page regarding the fundamental truths of their faith.

The process of deeper Bible study and theological exploration also fosters a spirit of humility and a recognition of our ongoing need for God's wisdom. As we delve into the vastness of God's truth, we inevitably encounter passages and concepts that challenge our current understanding or reveal the limitations of our own knowledge. This can be a humbling experience, but it is also one that drives us to rely more fully on the Holy Spirit to illuminate Scripture and guide our understanding. It teaches us that faith is not about having all the answers, but about continually seeking Him and trusting in His revelation. This disposition of humility is a vital characteristic for spiritual growth, both individually and as a family.

Finally, dedicating specific periods to this kind of intensive study can also serve as a powerful antidote to superficial faith. In a culture that often encourages quick fixes and surface-level engagement, deliberately choosing to invest time and effort in understanding biblical truths helps to build a more resilient and deeply rooted faith. It moves us beyond simply knowing "about" God to knowing Him more intimately. This rich engagement with Scripture and theology equips us to stand firm in our beliefs, to live out our faith with conviction, and to pass on a legacy of robust faith to future generations. It is an investment in the spiritual health and intellectual vitality of our family that yields eternal dividends.

The constant demands of family life, career, and the general hustle of modern living can, over time, create a subtle drift in the marital relationship. Like two ships sailing side-by-side, without deliberate adjustments to course, the distance between them can gradually widen. This is precisely why intentionally carving out time specifically for marital enrichment is not merely a luxury, but a vital necessity for the ongoing health and spiritual vitality of a marriage. Just as we recognize the need for regular spiritual refreshment for ourselves and our families, so too must we acknowledge the unique spiritual and relational needs of the partnership that forms the bedrock of the home. This proactive investment in the marital bond is a testament to our commitment to the covenant we have made and a powerful way to foster spiritual growth that impacts the entire household.

One of the most effective ways to achieve this intentional enrichment is through dedicated marriage retreats or getaways. These periods, whether a weekend at a quiet bed and breakfast, a longer stay at a Christian conference center, or even a carefully planned day at home devoid of typical distractions, offer a crucial opportunity to step away from the everyday and focus exclusively on each other and on strengthening the spiritual core of the marriage. The very act of physically removing oneself from the familiar routines and responsibilities creates a unique environment conducive to deeper connection. The absence of laundry piles, school schedules, work emails, and household chores liberates the couple from the mundane, allowing them to re-center their focus on the sacredness of their union. This deliberate pause allows for a recalibration of priorities, bringing the marriage back to the forefront of attention.

The benefits of such an intentional retreat are manifold. Firstly, it provides an unparalleled space for enhanced communication. When daily life is a constant barrage of to-do lists and logistical planning, conversations often become functional, revolving around who is picking up whom or what needs to be bought at the grocery store. A retreat, however, invites conversations that are deeper, more reflective, and more vulnerable. It allows couples to share their inner thoughts and feelings without the pressure of immediate interruptions or the need to rush to the next task. This could involve discussing dreams and aspirations that may have been put on hold, sharing concerns that have been weighing on the heart, or simply reminiscing about cherished memories that have bonded them. These kinds of conversations are the lifeblood of intimacy, fostering understanding and empathy, and rebuilding emotional closeness.

Spiritually, these focused times away can be incredibly transformative. Many marriage retreats are designed with a spiritual component, offering teachings, workshops, or guided devotionals that explore biblical principles for a healthy, God-honoring marriage. These sessions can provide fresh perspectives on biblical roles within marriage, equip couples with tools for conflict resolution rooted in grace and forgiveness, and deepen their understanding of God's design for their union. Imagine dedicating an afternoon to studying passages like Ephesians 5:22-33, discussing what it truly means for a wife to respect her husband and for a husband to love his wife sacrificially, as Christ loved the church. Such focused study, away from the distractions of everyday life, allows for deeper processing and application of God's Word to their specific marital context. It's an opportunity to intentionally align their marriage with God's purposes, strengthening their spiritual unity as a couple.

Furthermore, these getaways provide an opportunity to rekindle romance and intimacy. In the busyness of life, the physical and emotional intimacy within a marriage can sometimes take a backseat. A retreat offers a chance to deliberately prioritize this aspect of the relationship. It's about creating an environment where affection, tenderness, and open expression of love can flourish once again. This might involve intentional date nights during the retreat, prioritizing physical closeness, or simply making a conscious effort to speak words of affirmation and appreciation. When couples feel truly seen, heard, and cherished by their spouse, their bond is significantly strengthened. This renewed intimacy not only enhances their personal connection but also creates a more vibrant spiritual atmosphere within the home.

The process of planning and anticipating a retreat can also be a unifying experience. When both partners are actively involved in choosing a location, selecting activities, and setting intentions for the time away, it fosters a sense of shared purpose and excitement. This collaborative planning itself becomes an act of investment in the marriage. It's a tangible expression of commitment and a mutual desire to nurture their relationship. Even the simple act of packing for the trip together can be a small yet significant opportunity for connection.

When considering the types of retreats, there is a spectrum of options to suit different needs and budgets. A full-blown, professionally organized marriage conference can offer comprehensive teaching and structured activities. These often bring together expert speakers and provide a wealth of resources. Alternatively, a simpler weekend getaway to a scenic location can be just as effective, especially when couples commit to dedicating a significant portion of their time to intentional activities focused on their marriage. This might involve reading a marriage devotional together each morning, engaging in guided prayer for their relationship, or setting aside time each day for open, honest conversation. For those with very limited time or resources, a "staycation" retreat, where the home is transformed into a sanctuary for marital focus, can be a powerful solution. This involves consciously shutting out all external demands, perhaps by turning off phones, deferring non-essential chores, and creating a special atmosphere for connection. The key is not the location, but the intentionality and the dedicated focus on the marital relationship.

The spiritual dimension of these retreats is paramount. They are not simply about improving communication skills or rekindling romance, though those are valuable outcomes. At their core, these intentional times are about strengthening the marriage as a reflection of Christ's love for the Church. This involves seeking God's wisdom and guidance for their union, praying together for their individual and shared spiritual growth, and exploring how they can better serve God together as a couple. Many retreats offer opportunities for couples to be ministered to by seasoned Christian counselors or leaders, providing invaluable insights and support.

However, the impact of these retreats can extend far beyond the time spent away. The practices and insights gained during a retreat should ideally be integrated into the daily rhythms of married life. This means consciously continuing the practices of deep communication, regular spiritual connection, and intentional affection. A retreat can serve as a powerful catalyst, igniting a renewed commitment to prioritize the marriage on an ongoing basis. It's an investment that yields dividends long after the suitcases have been unpacked.

Consider the example of a couple who, feeling a sense of growing distance, decides to book a weekend marriage retreat. Upon arrival, they are immediately struck by the quiet and the absence of their usual responsibilities. The first evening, instead of defaulting to separate activities, they intentionally sit down with a marriage devotional. The topic is on forgiveness, and as they discuss the relevant scripture and reflection questions, long-held, unspoken hurts begin to surface. Through tears and honest conversation, facilitated by the calm environment and the shared focus, they find a path toward genuine forgiveness and reconciliation. The next day, they attend a session on spiritual intimacy, learning practical ways to pray together more effectively and to support each other's spiritual journeys. They leave the retreat not only feeling reconnected and refreshed but also equipped with new tools and a renewed commitment to nurture their marriage with intentionality.

Another important aspect to consider is the element of adventure and shared experience that often accompanies a getaway. Whether it's exploring a new town together, trying a new restaurant, or simply enjoying the beauty of nature, shared new experiences can create new memories and strengthen the bond between partners. These moments of shared enjoyment and discovery add another layer of richness to the marital connection. It's about creating a mosaic of shared experiences that are built upon the foundation of their shared faith and commitment.

The spiritual refreshment that comes from prioritizing the marriage is profound. When a marriage is strong, centered on Christ, and characterized by love, respect, and open communication, it creates a stable and nurturing environment for the entire family. Children raised in homes where the marital relationship is a priority, and where parents model healthy spiritual and relational dynamics, are more likely to develop a secure sense of belonging and to understand the importance of commitment and love. The intentional investment in the marriage is therefore an investment in the spiritual health and well-being of the entire family unit. It's a ripple effect, where the strengthening of the marital bond positively impacts every member of the household.

Moreover, these dedicated times away can help couples to address and resolve underlying issues that might be subtly eroding their connection. Without this intentional space, unresolved conflicts or unexpressed needs can fester, leading to resentment and emotional distance. A retreat, with its focus on open communication and biblical principles, can provide the ideal setting to confront these challenges in a healthy and constructive way. It's about creating a safe harbor where difficult conversations can be had, and healing can begin.

The choice of when to schedule these retreats is also important. It might be beneficial to plan one during a less demanding season of the year, or perhaps to coincide with a significant anniversary. However, it's also crucial to remember that these intentional times of enrichment should not be relegated to rare, extraordinary occasions. Even smaller, more frequent breaks can have a significant impact. A monthly dedicated "couple's time" at home, free from distractions, where they focus on a shared spiritual activity or a deep conversation, can be just as vital as a yearly getaway. The consistency of prioritizing the marriage is key.

Ultimately, marriage enrichment retreats or getaways are an outward expression of an inward commitment to cherish and nurture the covenant of marriage. They are a tangible demonstration that the marital relationship is a sacred trust, deserving of dedicated time, effort, and spiritual focus. By stepping away from the demands of daily life, couples create fertile ground for spiritual growth, deeper intimacy, and a more profound connection with each other and with God. This proactive investment is not about escaping reality, but about building a stronger, more resilient, and more Christ-centered marriage that can weather any storm and become a powerful testament to God's enduring love. The intentionality behind these times ensures that the marriage remains a vibrant, growing, and spiritually dynamic force within the family.

Beyond the vital focus on marital enrichment, nurturing the spiritual health of the entire family unit requires intentional periods of collective growth. Just as we recognize the need to periodically step away from the daily grind to refresh our individual spirits, so too must we seek out opportunities to immerse our families in shared spiritual experiences. These are not merely holidays or vacations in the conventional sense, but rather deliberate invitations to step into a sacred space, even if that space is a tent under the stars or a quiet corner of our own home, dedicated to deepening our shared walk with Christ. The aim is to create an atmosphere where faith is not just discussed, but lived and breathed together, forging bonds that are not only familial but deeply spiritual.

One profoundly effective way to achieve this is through family spiritual retreats. These can take many forms, tailored to your family's unique dynamics, ages, and interests. Consider the simple yet powerful act of a camping trip infused with spiritual purpose. Imagine setting up camp in a serene natural setting, far from the constant hum of electronics and the pressures of everyday schedules. The mornings can begin with a family devotion by the campfire, perhaps exploring a passage from Psalms that speaks of God's majesty in creation, or reading a children's Bible story that illustrates a timeless spiritual truth. As the day unfolds, activities can naturally lend themselves to spiritual reflection. A hike can become an opportunity to discuss God's handiwork in the intricate details of nature, fostering a sense of awe and wonder. Evenings, under a canopy of stars, can be dedicated to prayer together, lifting up individual needs and thanking God for His blessings. The shared tasks of setting up camp, cooking meals together, and simply enjoying each other's company in a relaxed environment can become acts of service and connection, mirroring the selfless love we are called to as Christians. The absence of distractions allows for deeper conversations, where children can openly ask questions about faith, and parents can share their own spiritual journeys and struggles, fostering an environment of authenticity and trust. These shared experiences in nature, when framed through a lens of faith, can create lasting memories and plant seeds of spiritual understanding that will continue to grow long after the tent is packed away.

Alternatively, your family retreat might involve a visit to a place of worship or spiritual significance. This could be a pilgrimage to a historic church, a monastery, or a site known for its spiritual resonance. The journey itself can be a time of anticipation and preparation, perhaps by listening to Christian podcasts or audiobooks in the car, or by engaging in family prayer for the trip ahead. Upon arrival, spend time soaking in the atmosphere of reverence. Attend a service, if possible, and allow the hymns, prayers, and scripture readings to minister to your souls collectively. Explore the architecture, learn about the history and the faith that has been expressed in that place for generations. Many such locations offer guided tours that delve into their spiritual significance, providing rich historical and theological context. Engage your children in observing the symbols and practices, explaining their meaning and connecting them to your own faith. This immersion in a tangible representation of faith can be incredibly powerful, helping children to understand that Christianity is not just an abstract concept but a living, breathing tradition with a deep and rich history. Such visits can also offer opportunities for quiet contemplation and personal prayer, allowing each family member to connect with God on a deeper level.

For families who may not be able to travel, or who prefer a more intimate setting, a dedicated weekend at home can be transformed into a powerful spiritual retreat. The key here is intentionality and the deliberate creation of a sacred space and time. Begin by communicating the plan to your family, perhaps a week or two in advance, framing it as a special "family faith-cation." Designate specific times for focused activities, ensuring that distractions are minimized. This might involve turning off televisions, silencing mobile phones (or designating specific "phone-free" times), and deferring non-essential household chores. The living room can be transformed into a prayer chapel, complete with comfortable seating, candles, and perhaps a cross or other religious symbols. Mornings could start with a shared breakfast followed by a scripture study. Choose a book of the Bible that is accessible and engaging for all ages, such as the Gospels or the book of Proverbs. Use age-appropriate study guides or simply engage in discussion, asking open-ended questions like, "What does this passage teach us about God?" or "How can we apply this to our lives this week?" Even young children can participate by drawing pictures related to the scripture or by memorizing short verses.

Prayer is another cornerstone of these at-home retreats. Dedicate specific times for corporate prayer. This could involve a "prayer chain" where each family member adds a prayer request for another family member, creating a tangible expression of mutual care and support. You might also try a structured prayer method, such as praying through the Lord's Prayer verse by verse, or using an acrostic for prayer, like ACTS (Adoration, Confession, Thanksgiving, Supplication). Encourage spontaneity and authenticity in prayer; it's not about eloquent speeches, but about heartfelt communication with God.

Consider incorporating elements of worship that are meaningful to your family. This might involve singing hymns or contemporary Christian songs together, perhaps with one family member leading the music on a piano or guitar, or simply using a worship playlist. You could also explore different forms of worship, such as creative expression through art or drama, using biblical stories as inspiration. The goal is to create an environment where worship is a joyous and shared experience, fostering a sense of unity in spirit.

Another valuable component of a family spiritual retreat, whether at home or away, is the opportunity for confession and reconciliation. Life within a family, however loving, inevitably involves moments of conflict and hurt. A retreat provides a dedicated space to address these issues in a spirit of grace and forgiveness, as modeled by Christ. Set aside time for each family member to share anything they feel they need to confess or apologize for, and for others to offer forgiveness. This practice, rooted in biblical principles (James 5:16), can be incredibly healing and strengthen the bonds of love within the family. It's a tangible way to demonstrate that forgiveness is a cornerstone of Christian living and a vital aspect of healthy family relationships.

The inclusion of service, even in a small way, can also enhance the spiritual impact of these times. This might involve preparing a meal for a neighbor, writing thank-you notes to missionaries your family supports, or engaging in a simple act of charity. When children see faith being lived out in practical ways, it reinforces the importance of compassion and generosity. It teaches them that faith is not just about what happens within the walls of the church or home, but also about how we impact the world around us.

When planning these retreats, remember to involve your children in the process. Ask for their input on activities, themes, or even locations. When children have a sense of ownership, they are more likely to be engaged and enthusiastic. This collaboration also provides a practical lesson in decision-making and compromise, further strengthening family unity. The anticipation itself can be a valuable spiritual discipline, building excitement for dedicated time with God and with each other.

The duration of these retreats can vary. A single day might be sufficient for a focused spiritual refresh, perhaps a Saturday dedicated to scripture, prayer, and a special family meal. A full weekend, from Friday evening to Sunday afternoon, offers a more immersive experience, allowing for a deeper dive into spiritual practices and more relaxed fellowship. For families with the means and the opportunity, a longer retreat, perhaps a week during a school break, can be even more transformative. Whatever the duration, the consistent element is the intentionality – the deliberate setting apart of time and space for spiritual growth as a family unit.

Furthermore, consider incorporating elements that allow for personal reflection alongside corporate activities. Provide journals for each family member to write down their thoughts, prayers, or insights gained during the retreat. This encourages personal engagement with the material and can be a valuable tool for ongoing spiritual growth. When children are encouraged to process their faith journey individually, it fosters independent spiritual thinking and a deeper personal relationship with God.

The spiritual impact of these collective experiences extends far beyond the retreat itself. The shared memories of singing worship songs around a campfire, of wrestling with a challenging Bible verse together, or of offering prayers for one another, create a spiritual tapestry that binds the family together. These are the moments that children will carry with them, shaping their understanding of faith and family for years to come. When families intentionally invest in these shared spiritual journeys, they are building a legacy of faith that can be passed down through generations, strengthening not only their present bonds but also their future connection to God and to one another. It's an investment in the eternal well-being of each family member and in the spiritual legacy of the household. The creation of these immersive experiences serves as a tangible expression of a family's commitment to prioritizing God in their lives, fostering a unity of purpose and a shared spiritual identity that will undoubtedly enrich their lives together.

The rhythm of spiritual growth within a home isn't a static melody; it's a dynamic symphony that requires our attentive conducting. Just as a skilled gardener regularly surveys their plants, checking for growth, signs of distress, or areas needing more attention, we as Christian wives and mothers must likewise set aside dedicated time to review and adjust our spiritual goals. This isn't a task to be approached with dread or a sense of obligation, but rather with eager anticipation, recognizing it as a vital opportunity to recalibrate our efforts and ensure we are faithfully walking the path God has laid out for our families. A monthly or at least quarterly assessment allows us to pause from the busyness of daily life and prayerfully consider where we are, where we're heading, and how best to get there.

The foundation of this review process is, without question, prayer. Before diving into any tangible assessment, we must first seek the wisdom and guidance of the Holy Spirit. Approaching this time with a heart that is open and teachable is paramount. We might begin by dedicating a specific quiet time, perhaps early in the morning before the household awakens, or during a tranquil afternoon, solely for this purpose. This isn't about listing personal accomplishments, but about seeking God's perspective on our family's spiritual journey. Questions to bring before Him include: "Lord, where have you seen our family's faith flourishing this past month?" or "Are there areas where we, as a family, have drifted or become complacent?" Inviting God into this process ensures that our adjustments are not based on our own limited understanding or earthly metrics, but on His divine will and purpose for our household.

Once we have surrendered the process to prayer, we can begin to engage in a more tangible review of our established spiritual goals. Think back to the goals we set at the beginning of the month or quarter. Were they specific, measurable, achievable, relevant, and time-bound (SMART goals, if you will, but infused with spiritual purpose)? For instance, if a goal was to read a specific book of the Bible together as a family, how did we fare? Did we manage to read it consistently, or did life's interruptions consistently derail our efforts? It's not about self-condemnation, but honest evaluation. Perhaps the goal was too ambitious for the season of life we are in, or perhaps the method we chose wasn't the most effective for our family's learning style. Celebrating even small victories is crucial. If we aimed to have family devotions three times a week and managed it twice, that's progress worth acknowledging and thanking God for. This positive reinforcement can be incredibly motivating as we move forward.

Consider the various facets of our family's spiritual life. This could include prayer, scripture study, corporate worship, acts of service, and the cultivation of godly character traits within each family member. For prayer, were we more consistent in praying together as a family? Did we establish a rhythm of prayer that felt natural and life-giving? If our goal was to incorporate specific prayer practices, like praying through the ACTS acronym (Adoration, Confession, Thanksgiving, Supplication) or using prayer journals, how did that experiment go? Sometimes, a particular method might resonate deeply, while another might feel forced. The review is the time to discern this. When it comes to scripture study, did we engage with the Word in a way that sparked curiosity and understanding, or did it feel like a dry academic exercise? Perhaps we need to explore different translations, use visual aids, or incorporate storytelling to bring the passages to life.

Our engagement with the broader Christian community also warrants review. Are we actively participating in our local church? Are we modeling for our children the importance of corporate worship and fellowship? Are we involved in opportunities to serve within the church body or in the wider community? If a goal was to volunteer for a specific outreach program or to regularly support a missionary family, assessing our commitment to these external expressions of faith is important. These outward actions often reflect the inward state of our spiritual lives and provide tangible ways for our families to live out their faith.

When we identify areas where we have fallen short of our goals, it's essential to approach these with grace and a willingness to adjust. This is not a time for discouragement, but for redirection. Life is unpredictable, and our families are dynamic entities. What worked perfectly last month might not be effective this month due to changing circumstances, new challenges, or even opportunities that arise. For example, if a family devotions time that was consistently scheduled for after dinner is now fraught with fatigue and distraction because of a child's new extracurricular activity, it might be time to shift that devotional time to earlier in the day or even to a weekend morning. Similarly, if a particular Bible study curriculum proved too complex for the younger children, a review might prompt a search for a more age-appropriate resource or a simplified approach.

Adjusting our strategies might also involve embracing new methods or resources. Perhaps we've been relying heavily on one particular approach to family worship, and we're noticing a dip in engagement. This review could be the catalyst to explore other avenues. Maybe it's time to introduce more music and singing, to explore faith-based board games, or to engage in creative activities like dramatizing Bible stories. The key is to remain flexible and responsive to the needs and spiritual receptivity of our family members. We are not bound to a rigid plan if God is clearly leading us in a different direction. The goal is effective spiritual nurturing, not adherence to a plan for its own sake.

Furthermore, this review process provides an excellent opportunity to assess the spiritual health and progress of individual family members. Are our children demonstrating a growing understanding of their faith? Are they exhibiting godly character traits like kindness, patience, and honesty in their daily interactions? Are they developing a personal prayer life? While we don't want to pry into their private conversations with God, we can observe their attitudes, their words, and their actions. We can also create space for them to share their spiritual thoughts and questions. Perhaps a child has been expressing a particular interest in a biblical figure, or a struggle with a specific sin. These insights are invaluable for tailoring our family's spiritual focus and for offering targeted encouragement and guidance.

It's also important to be honest about our own spiritual condition as mothers and wives. Are we modeling the faith we wish to instill? Are we prioritizing our personal relationship with God through prayer, scripture, and worship? Our own spiritual vitality is the wellspring from which our family's spiritual nourishment flows. If our personal spiritual life is waning, it will inevitably impact the entire household. Therefore, our review should also include an honest assessment of our own spiritual disciplines and a willingness to adjust our personal schedules and priorities to ensure we are continually drawing from the source of all life.

This monthly or quarterly review should not be a solitary exercise.

Ideally, it would involve our spouse. If you are married, discussing your observations and proposed adjustments with your husband is crucial. You are partners in this spiritual endeavor, and a unified approach strengthens the family's spiritual foundation. Sharing your insights, listening to his perspectives, and collectively agreeing on the path forward creates a powerful synergy. If you are a single parent, you might enlist the support of a trusted mentor, a spiritual leader, or a close Christian friend to offer prayer and accountability during this review process.

As we celebrate the progress made and prayerfully address the areas needing adjustment, we are essentially renewing our commitment to the overarching vision for our faith-filled home. This vision might be a simple desire to raise children who love and serve God, or a more complex aspiration to be a household that actively demonstrates Christ's love to the world. By regularly reviewing and adjusting our spiritual goals, we ensure that our daily efforts are always moving us closer to that divine destination. It's a continuous process of leaning into God's leading, adapting to the ever-changing landscape of family life, and steadfastly cultivating a rich, vibrant spiritual atmosphere within our homes. This intentionality is what transforms a house into a true haven of faith, where God's presence is not just acknowledged, but actively experienced and cherished by every member of the family.

The journey of faith, like any significant pursuit, is rarely a linear ascent. Instead, it is characterized by seasons, some vibrant and lush, others arid and seemingly barren. As Christian wives and mothers, we are uniquely positioned to experience the ebb and flow of spiritual vitality within our own lives and to witness it, or perhaps feel its absence, in our families. It is inevitable that we will encounter periods of spiritual dryness, those stretches where the familiar intimacy with God feels distant, prayer seems like an exercise in futility, and the vibrant colors of faith fade to a muted gray. Discouragement, a close companion to dryness, can creep in, whispering doubts about our effectiveness, our spiritual health, and even God's presence. These seasons are not a sign of failure, but a testament to the reality of spiritual warfare and the human condition. Understanding that these times are a normal, albeit challenging, part of our walk is the first step in navigating them with grace and resilience.

When these arid seasons descend, the temptation can be to withdraw, to cease the very disciplines that have sustained us in the past, believing them to be fruitless. However, Scripture consistently points us toward recommitting to the foundational practices of our faith, even when our feelings don't align with these actions. Think of it like a farmer who, despite a drought, continues to till the soil and sow seeds, trusting in the promise of future rain. Our spiritual disciplines – consistent prayer, diligent scripture reading, faithful worship, and community involvement – are not contingent on our emotional state but on our obedience and trust in God. During times of dryness, it can be incredibly beneficial to simplify our approach. Instead of lengthy, eloquent prayers, we might focus on simple, heartfelt cries to God: "Lord, have mercy," or "Jesus, I need you." Reading the Word might become less about in-depth study and more about immersing ourselves in passages that speak of God's unfailing love and faithfulness, even if it's just a few verses a day. The act of engaging with these spiritual tools, even when it feels like working against a strong current, keeps the channels of communication open and signals to our spirit that we are still committed to the journey.

One of the most powerful antidotes to spiritual dryness and discouragement is the intentional engagement with our Christian community. The body of Christ is designed to be a source of mutual encouragement, support, and spiritual nourishment. When we feel our own spiritual wellspring running dry, turning to fellow believers can provide the very refreshment we need. This doesn't necessarily mean bearing our deepest struggles with every acquaintance, but rather seeking out those with whom we have a trusted relationship, a spiritual mentor, or a close friend within our small group or church. Sharing, in a spirit of vulnerability and humility, that we are experiencing a season of spiritual difficulty can often elicit profound empathy and practical support. Others have walked similar paths and can offer encouragement, pray with us, and remind us of God's faithfulness through their own testimonies.

Remembering God's faithfulness is not merely a passive recollection; it is an active, deliberate act of faith. When our present circumstances feel bleak, it is essential to look back at God's track record in our lives and the lives of His people throughout history. The Psalms are replete with David's laments, his cries of distress and feelings of abandonment, yet these are almost always followed by declarations of trust and praise, rooted in his remembrance of God's past deliverance. As wives and mothers, we have our own testimonies of God's provision, protection, and faithfulness. Keeping a journal of answered prayers, significant spiritual moments, or times God has intervened in seemingly impossible situations can serve as a powerful reminder during dry spells. When we feel discouraged, opening this journal and reading through these accounts can rekindle hope and faith, reinforcing the truth that the God who was faithful then is the same God who is with us now.

Moreover, it's vital to understand that spiritual growth,

paradoxically, often occurs in the very midst of struggle and perceived barrenness. Just as a sapling needs to withstand storms to develop strong roots, our faith is often forged and strengthened through periods of trial. When we persevere through spiritual dryness, choosing to obey God and engage in His prescribed means of grace even when we don't feel like it, we are developing spiritual muscles. We learn to rely on God's promises rather than our feelings, and we gain a deeper understanding of His sovereignty and His unwavering love. This perseverance builds endurance and a deeper, more resilient faith that can withstand future challenges. It is in these quiet battles, fought in prayer and obedience, that we often discover a deeper wellspring of God's strength within us, a strength that is not dependent on our outward circumstances but on our inward commitment to Him.

The concept of spiritual warfare is not abstract; it is a very real aspect of our Christian walk. The enemy of our souls actively seeks to discourage us, to sow seeds of doubt, and to create spiritual barrenness in our lives. Recognizing that periods of dryness might be a spiritual attack can help us to approach them with a more discerning and prayerful mindset. This doesn't mean attributing every difficult feeling to demonic influence, but rather acknowledging that there is an adversarial force that seeks to hinder our relationship with God and our effectiveness in Him. When we feel spiritually depleted, a renewed focus on putting on the full armor of God, as described in Ephesians 6, can be incredibly empowering. This includes the belt of truth, the breastplate of righteousness, the shoes of the gospel of peace, the shield of faith, the helmet of salvation, and the sword of the Spirit, which is the Word of God. Engaging with these spiritual weapons can help us to actively push back against discouragement and reclaim the ground that the enemy seeks to take.

When experiencing spiritual dryness, it's also beneficial to examine our personal lives for any unconfessed sin or areas of disobedience that might be hindering our intimacy with God. The Bible is clear that sin creates a separation between us and God. A period of spiritual drought can be a prompt from the Holy Spirit to examine our hearts and lives, confessing any known sin and seeking His forgiveness and cleansing. This is not a path to self-condemnation, but rather to renewed fellowship and spiritual vitality. As believers, we have access to the cleansing power of Christ through confession, and the assurance of His forgiveness. This can be a difficult but ultimately liberating step in overcoming spiritual dryness.

Furthermore, actively seeking to serve others, even when we feel spiritually weak, can sometimes be a catalyst for renewed spiritual vigor. When we shift our focus from our internal struggles to outward acts of love and service, we often find that God uses these moments to replenish our own spiritual reserves. This might involve bringing a meal to a struggling neighbor, volunteering at a local soup kitchen, or simply offering a word of encouragement to a friend. In giving, we often receive. In pouring out our spiritual and emotional energy into serving others, we can find that God refills us, reminding us of His purpose and His strength that flows through us, even when we feel depleted. It's a testament to God's grace that He can use us and sustain us even in our weakest moments.

Finding renewed strength in God's presence is the ultimate goal during seasons of dryness. This presence is not always felt in a dramatic, emotional surge, but can be found in the quiet, consistent reality of God's character and His promises. It is in remembering that God is always with us, even when we don't feel His presence strongly. He is the same yesterday, today, and forever. His love for us is unchanging, and His power is not diminished by our feelings of weakness. This truth can be a powerful anchor. We can also cultivate a deeper reliance on the Holy Spirit, the Comforter and Helper, who indwells believers. Praying for the Spirit's filling, asking Him to refresh our souls and to grant us a renewed sense of God's presence, can be a pivotal part of overcoming dryness.

As mothers, we are also called to be sensitive to the spiritual needs of our children. When we are experiencing dryness, it can be challenging to impart spiritual vitality to them. However, our faithful, albeit imperfect, commitment to God during these times can still be a powerful testimony. Our children can learn from our perseverance. They can witness our reliance on prayer, our turning to Scripture, and our engagement with the community, even when we are not feeling at our peak. Moreover, our own vulnerability can create opportunities for open conversations about faith and doubt. Sharing in an age-appropriate way that sometimes mommy feels far from God, but that she is choosing to trust Him anyway, can teach them valuable lessons about the nature of faith.

The key to navigating these challenging seasons is a persistent, unyielding commitment to Christ, not based on fleeting emotions, but on the solid foundation of His Word and His character. It's about choosing faith over feelings, obedience over inclination, and community over isolation. These periods of dryness are not a sign that God has abandoned us, but rather an invitation to lean more deeply into Him, to trust His faithfulness when our own feels inadequate, and to persevere with the hope that spring will always follow winter, and that God's grace is sufficient for every season of our lives.

The tapestry of a thriving Christian life, particularly for us as wives and mothers, is woven with threads of personal devotion, but its true strength and vibrancy are often revealed when intertwined with the lives of fellow believers. The journey we undertake is not meant to be a solitary expedition through spiritual landscapes; rather, it is a communal pilgrimage. While the previous sections have touched upon the internal disciplines necessary for sustaining our faith, it is equally crucial to recognize the profound impact of an outward-facing commitment to a supportive Christian community. This is where the resilience we cultivate in private finds its amplification, and where the challenges that can sometimes feel overwhelming are met with shared strength and divine wisdom.

The essence of Christian fellowship, or
koinonia, as it is known in the New Testament, is far more than mere social gathering; it is a profound sharing in Christ and in one another's lives, encompassing spiritual, emotional, and practical dimensions. When we are navigating the often-demanding seasons of motherhood and marriage, this koinonia becomes not just beneficial, but a lifeline. Imagine the solitary farmer tending his fields under a harsh sun, battling pests and weather alone. Now, envision that same farmer working alongside others, sharing tools, knowledge, and encouragement. The labor is still demanding, but the burden is lightened, the challenges are more manageable, and the harvest feels more attainable because of the shared effort. So too it is with our spiritual journey. When discouragement looms, or when the sheer weight of responsibilities threatens to pull us under, the presence of a loving, praying community can be the very thing that lifts our heads and renews our strength.

This vibrant community can manifest in various forms, each offering unique blessings. Small groups, Bible study circles, women's ministry events, or even informal gatherings with like-minded sisters in Christ all serve as crucial conduits for mutual edification. Within these circles, we find the freedom to be truly known, to shed the masks of perfection that society, and sometimes even we ourselves, impose. It is in sharing our genuine struggles – the fatigue that settles deep into our bones, the anxieties that whisper doubts about our mothering or wifely capabilities, the moments of spiritual wrestling – that we discover we are not alone. Often, the very things we feel most ashamed of or isolated by are the common threads that bind us together, creating an immediate sense of empathy and understanding. When a sister in Christ can look you in the eye and say, "I've been there," or "I'm there now, and God is teaching me through it," it validates our experience and opens the door for healing and hope.

Beyond mere validation, a strong Christian community provides invaluable wisdom and perspective. As we juggle the diverse roles of wife, mother, homemaker, and often, perhaps, even a professional, our vision can become myopic. We can get so caught up in the day-to-day minutiae that we lose sight of the larger spiritual narrative. Fellow believers, with their own unique insights and experiences, can offer us a broader perspective. They can remind us of God's sovereignty, point out biblical principles we might be overlooking, or offer practical advice gleaned from their own journeys. A seasoned mother might share a strategy for managing toddler tantrums that has brought her peace, or a wife who has navigated marital challenges might offer counsel rooted in prayer and a deep understanding of God's design for marriage. This exchange of wisdom is a powerful tool in our arsenal for maintaining momentum, ensuring that our efforts are aligned with God's will and that we are growing in our understanding and application of His Word.

Mentorship, a vital component of spiritual community, deserves particular attention. Every stage of our Christian walk, from the early days of fledgling faith to seasoned years of spiritual maturity, benefits from the guiding hand of someone further along the path. For wives and mothers, this can mean having an older, wiser woman who has successfully navigated similar seasons. A spiritual mentor can provide a safe space to ask those "naïve" questions that we might be hesitant to voice in larger groups. She can offer encouragement when we feel like giving up, celebrate our victories with genuine joy and gently correct us when we stray off course, all with the unwavering love of Christ. The insights gained from a mentor can be transformative, offering a roadmap through the complexities of life and faith, helping us to avoid pitfalls and to embrace opportunities for growth with greater confidence and clarity. These relationships are not about hierarchy, but about the organic flow of spiritual life within the body of Christ, where those who have been blessed with experience can impart that blessing to others.

Accountability is another cornerstone of a healthy spiritual support system. In the context of our faith journey, accountability is not about judgment or condemnation, but about shared commitment and mutual encouragement to live in accordance with God's Word. When we are transparent with a trusted sister or a small group about our goals – perhaps to pray daily for our family, to dedicate more time to reading Scripture, or to cultivate a more Christ-like attitude in our homes – we create a layer of accountability that makes achieving those goals more likely. Knowing that others are praying for us and will gently inquire about our progress can be a powerful motivator. This accountability fosters a sense of responsibility not only to ourselves but to God and to the community that is cheering us on. It's a beautiful interplay where we are strengthened by the faith of others, and in turn, our perseverance can become a source of strength for them.

The importance of seeking out and actively cultivating this kind of spiritual network cannot be overstated. It requires intentionality. In our busy lives, spiritual community doesn't often just *happen*. We must actively seek it out, invest time and energy into it, and be willing to be vulnerable and open. This might mean making a conscious effort to attend church events, join a small group, or initiate coffee dates with women from our congregation. It means prioritizing these relationships, understanding that they are not a luxury but a necessity for spiritual well-being and sustained momentum. It also means being discerning about the communities we join. We are looking for environments that are rooted in biblical truth, characterized by genuine love, and foster spiritual growth. A community that is overly critical, gossipy, or lacks a genuine commitment to Christ will not provide the support we need and can, in fact, be detrimental.

As Christian wives and mothers, our spiritual resilience is not only for our own benefit but also has a ripple effect on our families. When we are spiritually strong, supported, and encouraged, we are better equipped to lead our homes with grace, patience, and a Christ-centered perspective. Our children and husbands benefit directly from our connection to the body of Christ, witnessing firsthand the transforming power of God's love at work through His people. They see us supported, they see us supporting others, and they learn that faith is not an isolated experience but a shared reality. This communal aspect of faith is a powerful testimony to the world around us, demonstrating that the love and grace of God are not abstract concepts but living, breathing realities that impact our everyday lives and relationships.

Moreover, this robust community acts as a vital buffer against the isolation that can creep into our homes, particularly for mothers who spend significant time within the domestic sphere. The daily rhythms of childcare and homemaking, while fulfilling, can sometimes lead to a feeling of being disconnected from the broader world and even from other believers. A supportive community provides an essential antidote to this isolation, ensuring that we maintain vital connections with others who understand and share our spiritual journey. It offers opportunities for meaningful conversation, shared laughter, and mutual prayer that can revitalize our spirits and remind us of the larger purpose to which we are called. It's about being part of something bigger than ourselves, a divine tapestry where each of us plays a crucial role.

In essence, the proactive cultivation and engagement with a supportive Christian community is not an optional add-on to our faith; it is an integral part of maintaining momentum on this lifelong journey. It is in the warmth of genuine fellowship, the wisdom of shared experience, the guidance of mentors, and the strength of accountability that we find the resilience to press on, to grow deeper in our love for Christ, and to effectively nurture our families in His truth. When we are part of a healthy, vibrant Christian community, we are never truly alone in our struggles or in our triumphs, and this shared journey is a testament to the abundant life God promises to all who follow Him. It is a divine provision designed to sustain us, encourage us, and ultimately, to bring greater glory to His name through our lives and through our homes. It is a sanctuary where our spirits can be refreshed, our faith can be strengthened, and our love for God and one another can flourish.

The journey of faith, much like the art of homemaking, is not a static achievement but a dynamic process of continuous growth and refinement. Just as a well-tended garden requires ongoing attention, soil enrichment, and thoughtful pruning to flourish, so too does our spiritual life necessitate a steadfast commitment to learning and development. To maintain momentum, we must actively pursue avenues that deepen our understanding of God's Word and His will for our lives, ensuring our faith remains vibrant, relevant, and empowering amidst the ever-changing landscape of family life and personal development. This is not about reaching a destination, but about embracing the rich, transformative journey itself, allowing each season to equip us with greater wisdom and grace.

One of the most accessible and powerful tools for continuing personal spiritual growth is the vast treasury of Christian literature. The written word, penned by men and women who have wrestled with faith, have experienced profound encounters with God, and have diligently studied Scripture, offers a unique opportunity for discipleship. Engaging with well-crafted theological works, insightful commentaries, and inspiring biographies can illuminate complex biblical truths, provide practical guidance for navigating life's challenges, and reignite our passion for Christ. Consider the early church fathers, whose writings still resonate with profound spiritual depth, or the reformers, whose unwavering commitment to Scripture continues to inspire. Today, a wealth of contemporary authors addresses the specific needs and questions faced by women in their roles as wives, mothers, and homemakers. Books exploring biblical perspectives on marriage, parenting from a faith-based viewpoint, or devotional guides that offer daily encouragement can be invaluable resources. Dedicating even a small portion of our week to reading—perhaps during a quiet morning before the household awakens, or during a stolen moment while children nap—can yield significant spiritual dividends. It is a quiet investment that pays rich rewards, sharpening our minds, nurturing our souls, and grounding our faith in the timeless truths of God's Word.

Beyond individual study, the structured learning offered through Christian courses and workshops provides an excellent framework for deeper engagement. Many churches and Christian organizations offer Bible studies, theological classes, or topical seminars designed to equip believers for various aspects of Christian living. These environments often foster a sense of community, allowing for shared learning, discussion, and mutual encouragement. When we commit to a course, we are not only absorbing new information but also dedicating ourselves to a period of focused spiritual discipline. This could be an in-depth study of a particular book of the Bible, an exploration of Christian apologetics, or a practical workshop on cultivating a Christ-centered home. Such programs can provide the structure and accountability needed to move beyond superficial understanding to a more profound grasp of God's truth. The interaction with instructors and fellow students can also offer diverse perspectives, challenging our assumptions and broadening our spiritual horizons in ways that solitary study might not.

Attending Christian conferences and retreats represents another vital aspect of sustained spiritual education. These events, often featuring gifted speakers, worship leaders, and opportunities for corporate prayer, are designed to immerse attendees in an environment of spiritual renewal and impartation. They offer a unique chance to step away from the demands of daily life and focus exclusively on spiritual matters. The concentrated time spent in teaching, worship, and fellowship can be incredibly invigorating, rekindling a sense of purpose and re-energizing our commitment to Christ. Many women find that the inspiration gained at a conference can fuel their faith and service for months afterward. Furthermore, conferences often provide practical tools and strategies for applying biblical principles to everyday life, empowering us to be more effective in our homes and more impactful in our spheres of influence. The opportunity to connect with like-minded women from different backgrounds can also be a source of immense encouragement and broaden our understanding of the global body of Christ.

The pursuit of spiritual growth is intrinsically linked to intellectual engagement. Our faith is not meant to be a blind leap but a reasoned trust, grounded in the truth of God's Word and His character. Therefore, continuing our education in matters of faith is essential for maintaining a robust and resilient Christianity. As Christian wives and mothers, we are called to be disciples who not only believe but also understand and can articulate the hope that is within us. This requires a willingness to ask questions, to grapple with difficult passages of Scripture, and to seek out reliable sources of theological understanding. It means being discerning consumers of information, evaluating teachings and resources against the unchanging standard of God's Word. By actively engaging our minds in the study of God's truth, we fortify our faith against doubt and deception, and we equip ourselves to lead our families with a clear, biblically-informed vision. This commitment to lifelong learning ensures that our faith remains a living, breathing reality, capable of guiding us through every season of life with grace, wisdom, and unwavering hope.

The practical application of our faith in the realm of homemaking, marriage, and parenting is profoundly impacted by our ongoing spiritual education. When we understand God's design for these foundational aspects of life, we can approach them with greater purpose and effectiveness. Learning about biblical principles of hospitality, for instance, can transform our homes into places of warmth and welcome, reflecting God's own generous nature. Studying Scripture on effective communication and conflict resolution can strengthen our marriages, fostering intimacy and mutual respect. Gaining insight into child-rearing from a godly perspective equips us to nurture our children's spiritual development, guiding them toward a lifelong relationship with Christ. Each of these areas benefits immensely from dedicated study and a willingness to grow. As our children mature and our marriages evolve, the demands and challenges we face will also change. A commitment to ongoing spiritual learning ensures that we are not caught off guard but are consistently equipped with the wisdom and understanding needed to navigate these transitions with grace and faithfulness. This proactive approach prevents spiritual stagnation and allows us to continually discover new depths of God's provision for every aspect of our lives.

Furthermore, embracing lifelong learning in our faith journey helps us to remain spiritually vibrant and relevant. A static faith can quickly become a stale faith, susceptible to apathy or legalism. By actively seeking to learn and grow, we keep our spiritual lives dynamic and exciting. We discover new dimensions of God's character, encounter His truth in fresh ways, and are continually inspired to live more fully for Him. This pursuit of knowledge and understanding is not merely an academic exercise; it is an act of worship, a response to the boundless love and wisdom of our Creator. It allows us to continually renew our minds, as the Apostle Paul encourages us in Romans 12:2, transforming us from the inside out. This transformation is what enables us to meet the evolving demands of family life not with weariness, but with a renewed sense of purpose and an abiding confidence in God's sustaining power.

The availability of resources today is truly remarkable. Online courses, digital libraries, reputable Christian websites, and podcasts offer an almost limitless array of learning opportunities, accessible from the comfort of our homes. We can listen to sermons from esteemed preachers while doing household chores, engage with in-depth Bible study modules during our commute, or access theological discussions on demand. This accessibility is a tremendous blessing, enabling us to integrate spiritual learning seamlessly into our busy lives. The key is intentionality. We must make a conscious decision to prioritize these resources, to carve out time for them, and to approach them with a teachable spirit. It's about recognizing that investing in our spiritual growth is as important, if not more important, than any other pursuit.

Consider the impact of staying intellectually engaged with our faith on our children. When they see their mothers actively seeking to understand and live out their faith, it provides a powerful example. They witness firsthand that Christianity is not a set of rules to be followed passively, but a dynamic, living relationship with God that requires ongoing growth and exploration. This can inspire them to develop their own hunger for God's Word and to seek Him for themselves. Our personal commitment to learning becomes a catalyst for intergenerational faith. It demonstrates that faith is a journey, not a destination, and that there are always new depths to explore and new ways to grow closer to God. This active pursuit of knowledge also equips us to answer their inevitable questions about faith with greater depth and assurance, building a foundation of biblical understanding within our homes.

In summary, the commitment to continuing personal spiritual growth and education is not an optional add-on but a foundational element for maintaining momentum on the lifelong journey of faith. By availing ourselves of the rich array of resources—from literature and structured courses to conferences and digital media—and by approaching our spiritual development with intentionality and a teachable spirit, we ensure that our faith remains vibrant, relevant, and empowering. This ongoing investment equips us to navigate the complexities of homemaking, marriage, and parenting with increasing wisdom, grace, and effectiveness, while also providing a powerful testament to the transformative power of God's truth for our families and for the world around us. It is in this continuous pursuit of Him that we find the strength to press on, to flourish, and to bring glory to His name through every aspect of our lives.

The journey of faith, once begun, is never truly complete. It is a lifelong pilgrimage, marked by seasons of growth, challenges, and, most importantly, by the beautiful and vital task of passing on the enduring legacy of our Christian heritage. As we ourselves strive to maintain spiritual momentum, a significant part of that momentum is channeled into nurturing the next generation. This isn't merely about imparting knowledge or instilling good habits; it is about the profound and deliberate act of discipleship, intentionally guiding our children to develop their own personal, vibrant faith in Christ. This process is the heart of maintaining spiritual momentum not just for ourselves, but for the continuity of God's work in our family lineage.

Discipling our children is a sacred trust, a mandate woven into the fabric of Christian family life. It begins not at some arbitrary age, but from the earliest moments of their lives, laying the groundwork with foundational spiritual training. This early stage involves familiarizing them with God's love through simple stories, songs, and prayers. It's about creating an atmosphere in our homes where faith is not an abstract concept, but a lived reality. As they grow, this foundation expands. We transition from simply sharing biblical narratives to actively teaching them how to engage with Scripture themselves. This could involve memorizing key verses, using age-appropriate Bible translations, and teaching them how to look for God's character and His promises within the text. The goal is to cultivate in them a personal connection with God, one that is not solely dependent on what they hear from us, but on what they discover for themselves. We aim to equip them with the tools to approach God directly, to learn to listen to the Holy Spirit's quiet promptings, and to discern His will for their lives.

The development of a child's faith is intrinsically linked to their ability to make godly choices. This requires more than just teaching them right from wrong; it involves helping them understand the 'why' behind biblical principles. When a decision needs to be made, we can walk them through the process of considering biblical wisdom, praying for guidance, and evaluating potential outcomes through a spiritual lens. For instance, when faced with peer pressure to engage in an activity that conflicts with their values, the discipling process encourages them to recall Scripture that speaks to purity, integrity, or wisdom. It's about empowering them to say "no" to temptation not out of fear of punishment, but out of a deep-seated desire to honor God and to live in a way that reflects His character. This cultivates internal conviction, a crucial element for navigating the complexities of the world. As they practice making these choices, and as we offer gentle correction and affirmation, they build confidence in their ability to live a life pleasing to God. This builds a resilient faith that can withstand the inevitable challenges and temptations of life.

A significant aspect of this discipling process is the gradual shift from parental guidance to personal ownership of faith. As children mature, our role evolves from direct instruction to mentorship and encouragement. We want to see them not just obeying us, but actively pursuing God for themselves. This means creating opportunities for them to serve, to share their faith with others, and to lead in age-appropriate ways. Perhaps they can lead a family devotional, teach a younger sibling a Bible verse, or participate in a community service project that allows them to be a tangible expression of Christ's love. These experiences are invaluable for building their confidence and demonstrating their capacity to influence others for good. We are essentially preparing them to eventually "carry the torch" of faith, not just to hold onto it. This involves fostering a sense of responsibility and stewardship over the spiritual gifts and understanding God has given them. We want them to understand that faith is not a passive inheritance but an active, dynamic relationship that they are called to nurture and share.

The "torch" of faith that we pass on is not a flimsy candle easily extinguished, but a flame ignited by the Holy Spirit, sustained by God's Word, and fanned by intentional discipleship. This legacy of faith is built brick by brick, conversation by conversation, prayer by prayer. It's in the quiet moments of bedtime stories that echo with biblical truth, in the shared laughter during family worship, and in the honest conversations about life's struggles where faith is demonstrated. We are not just raising children; we are investing in the continuation of God's redemptive story. This means understanding that their faith journey will have its unique path. There will be times of fervent growth and perhaps times of questioning or wavering. Our role is to be a steadfast presence, offering grace, wisdom, and unwavering support, pointing them back to the unchanging truth of God's Word and the unfailing love of Christ.

The ultimate aim of this intergenerational discipleship is to equip our children to become mature believers who can then disciple others. This is the essence of spiritual momentum carrying forward. When our children internalize the principles of faith, develop a deep and personal relationship with Jesus, and learn the importance of making Godly choices, they are naturally positioned to influence those around them. They become living testimonies to the power of a faith that is lived out daily. This might manifest in their friendships at school, their future marriages and families, their professional lives, and their involvement in the church community. They become instruments of God's grace, sharing the hope and truth they have received. This outflowing of faith is the ultimate fulfillment of our discipling efforts, ensuring that the legacy we have been entrusted with continues to shine brightly, impacting lives for generations to come. It is a testament to the enduring power of God and the faithfulness of parents who prioritize His calling in their lives.

The foundational spiritual training we provide throughout childhood is not merely a preparatory phase; it is the very bedrock upon which their adult faith will be built and sustained. When children are immersed in an environment where prayer is natural, where Scripture is revered and studied, and where love for God and others is actively demonstrated, they internalize these values. This creates a deeply ingrained understanding of God's principles, which becomes a compass for their decisions as adults. For example, a child who has consistently seen their parents engage in honest communication, even during conflict, will be better equipped to navigate marital challenges themselves. Likewise, a child who has been taught the importance of generosity and service will likely carry that into their adult lives, impacting their communities positively. This isn't about perfection in parenting, but about consistent effort and a genuine desire to lead them to Christ.

To truly empower children to develop their own personal faith, we must resist the urge to live their faith for them. This means allowing them space to wrestle with questions, to experience conviction, and to make intentional choices about their beliefs and practices. It involves moving beyond simply telling them what to believe, to fostering an environment where they can explore and discover God's truth for themselves. This might look like encouraging them to lead a Bible study within their peer group, supporting their desire to volunteer for a ministry, or simply providing them with resources that challenge and deepen their understanding of God. When we trust God to work in their hearts and minds, and when we trust the spiritual foundation we have laid, we empower them to become resilient, independent believers who are not easily swayed by the fluctuating currents of the world.

The responsibility to disciple the next generation is a weighty one, but it is also a privilege overflowing with divine promise. As we pour our lives into nurturing young believers, we are participating in God's eternal plan. We are ensuring that the light of the Gospel continues to shine, passed from one generation to the next. This is the essence of maintaining spiritual momentum—not just for ourselves, but for the ongoing work of God's kingdom. The enduring legacy of faith within our families is a testament to God's faithfulness and a powerful witness to a watching world. It is a journey that requires patience, perseverance, and a deep reliance on the Holy Spirit, but the eternal rewards, both for our children and for the glory of God, are immeasurable. Our commitment to this sacred task reflects our own devotion and ensures that the faith that has so richly blessed us will continue to bless generations to come.

Our lives, infused with faith and guided by love, are not meant to exist in a vacuum. Each day, as we navigate the responsibilities of homemaking, marriage, and motherhood, we are actively weaving a tapestry whose threads extend far beyond our present sight. This isn't merely about the daily routines or the tangible accomplishments; it is about the unseen, yet profoundly impactful, work of building a legacy. A legacy of faith is a deliberate and ongoing inheritance, one that is passed down not through mere possession, but through lived experience, consistent devotion, and unwavering commitment to God's truth. It is the quiet whisper of faith in the mundane, the steadfast prayer in the storm, and the radiant joy that emanates from a heart anchored in Christ. This enduring influence shapes not only our immediate family but also echoes through the corridors of time, touching lives we may never personally encounter.

Consider the foundational impact of a home where God's presence is palpable. This isn't about achieving a picture-perfect aesthetic or flawless execution of every task, but about cultivating an atmosphere where Christ is honored, His Word is cherished, and love is the prevailing language. When our homes are centers of grace, hospitality, and spiritual vitality, they become beacons of hope in a world often shrouded in darkness. The fragrance of faith within our walls has the power to permeate the lives of our children, our spouses, and even those who cross our thresholds. This intentional cultivation of a faith-filled environment is a profound act of stewardship, ensuring that the spiritual riches we have received are faithfully transmitted. It's in the simple act of gathering for family prayer, the shared anticipation of reading a beloved biblical story, or the honest conversations about spiritual struggles and triumphs that the bedrock of a lasting legacy is laid. These are the moments that engrave God's truth upon the hearts of the next generation, preparing them to carry the torch of faith forward with conviction.

Living a legacy of faith means embracing intentionality in every aspect of our lives. It is about recognizing that our choices, our attitudes, and our actions are not isolated events but contribute to a cumulative narrative. As wives and mothers, we are the chief architects of our homes, and the design we imprint upon them will speak volumes for years to come. This intentionality extends to nurturing our marriages, fostering deep and abiding love that reflects Christ's love for the Church. It means committing to open communication, mutual respect, and a shared pursuit of spiritual growth with our husbands. When our marriages are strong and God-honoring, they become a powerful testament to the transformative power of Christ, providing a stable and loving environment for our children to thrive. This marital foundation is a crucial component of the legacy we build, demonstrating to our children the beauty and sanctity of a covenant relationship.

Furthermore, our role as mothers extends beyond the physical nurturing of our children; it is a sacred calling to disciple them in the ways of faith. This process begins from the earliest moments, imbuing their lives with the knowledge of God's love through songs, stories, and simple prayers. As they grow, we continue to guide them, teaching them to engage with Scripture, to discern God's voice, and to make choices that honor Him. This is not about raising perfect children, but about raising children who have a personal relationship with Jesus, who understand His grace, and who are equipped to navigate the world with biblical wisdom. The discipleship we offer is a vital link in the chain of faith, ensuring that the spiritual inheritance we have received is not only preserved but amplified through their lives.

The legacy we leave is not solely measured by grand gestures or public declarations, but by the quiet, consistent devotion that characterizes our daily lives. It is found in the faithful tending of our homes, creating spaces that are not only orderly and beautiful but are also filled with peace and spiritual significance. A well-ordered home, managed with diligence and a spirit of thanksgiving, reflects a heart that is ordered by God. This includes the intentionality with which we approach meal preparation, the care we put into creating a welcoming atmosphere, and the effort we make to foster meaningful connections within our families. These seemingly small acts, when performed with a heart focused on honoring God, contribute to a powerful and enduring legacy. They communicate to our children that our faith is not confined to Sunday mornings but is woven into the fabric of our everyday existence.

The impact of a faith-filled home can be profound and far-reaching. It becomes a sanctuary, a place of refuge and strength, where individuals can return and be reminded of God's unfailing love and faithfulness. This legacy of hope is not limited to our immediate family; it has the potential to influence friends, extended family, and even the wider community. When our homes exude the aroma of Christ, they become places where others can encounter His presence and experience His transforming power. This outward expression of our faith, stemming from the intentional stewardship of our homes and families, is a tangible demonstration of God's grace at work. It's a testament to the truth that a life lived in devotion to Him can create ripples of blessing that extend far beyond our own lives.

We must also consider the inheritance we pass down through our words and our prayers. The encouragement we offer, the wisdom we impart, and the prayers we lift up for our loved ones are all integral components of our legacy. When we speak life and truth into our families, when we consistently point them to Christ, we are actively building a foundation of faith that will sustain them through all seasons of life. Our prayers are a powerful force, shaping the spiritual landscape of our families and interceding for their well-being and their walk with God. This legacy of prayer is a testament to our reliance on Him and our deep love for those entrusted to our care.

As we reflect on the journey of maintaining spiritual momentum, it becomes clear that this momentum is inextricably linked to the legacy we are actively creating. Our commitment to God, our dedication to our families, and our faithful stewardship of all that He has given us are not merely personal pursuits; they are acts of obedience that contribute to a grander narrative of His redemptive work. A home rooted in God's love and truth becomes a beacon, illuminating the path for future generations. It is a living testament to the enduring power of faith and a powerful witness to a watching world. Through intentionality, devotion, and a deep reliance on the Holy Spirit, we can ensure that the legacy we leave is one that brings glory to God and continues to impact lives for His kingdom, now and for eternity. This ongoing process of building a legacy is not a burden, but a privilege, an opportunity to participate in God's eternal plan and to leave an inheritance of faith that truly matters.

Afterward

I am deeply grateful to the Lord Jesus Christ, my Savior and Redeemer, for the wisdom, inspiration, and strength He has continually poured into my life. This book is a testament to His grace and the calling He has placed on my heart to encourage and equip fellow wives and mothers in their spiritual journeys and homemaking.

To my loving husband, thank you for your unwavering support, your constant encouragement, and your partnership in building our faith-filled home. Your faith, love, and prayers are a foundation upon which I stand.

To my precious children, you are the inspiration behind so many of the thoughts and reflections in these pages. Thank you for your patience, your joy, and for being the living embodiment of the legacy we strive to build.

I also want to express my sincere thanks to my cherished friends and family, whose lives and faith have been a constant source of encouragement and inspiration. Your prayers and belief in me have sustained me throughout this process.

Finally, I am thankful for the opportunity to share these reflections with you, and I pray that this book serves as a blessing and a tool for your own spiritual growth and the flourishing of your homes.

About the Author

Born and raised in a home that valued faith and family, Madison Weatherly has cultivated a lifelong passion for nurturing a Christian home. As a devoted wife and mother, she has experienced firsthand the profound joys and challenges of integrating faith into the everyday rhythm of domestic life. Her journey has been marked by a deep commitment to spiritual growth, a love for creating a warm and welcoming home, and a desire to pass on a lasting legacy of faith to her children.

With a background in writing, Madison brings a thoughtful and practical approach to exploring the intersection of faith, family, and homemaking. Her writing is characterized by its warmth, authenticity, and encouragement, drawing from personal experiences and a solid foundation in biblical principles. She believes that ordinary moments in the home hold extraordinary potential for spiritual impact and that every wife and mother is uniquely positioned to build a legacy that honors God.

Madison resides with her husband and children. When she is not writing or tending to her home, she enjoys reading, gardening and hiking with her husband. She prays that this book will be a source of inspiration and practical guidance for all who seek to deepen their faith and strengthen their families.